WAAS REVISED

G P S
M A D E
E A S Y

Using Global

Positioning

Systems in

the Outdoors

FOURTH EDITION

THE MOUNTAINEERS BOOKS

For Tanya
The only thing left to map is life,
and that only in retrospect

 Published by
The Mountaineers
1001 SW Klickitat Way, Suite 201
Seattle, WA 98134

GPS Made Easy, 4th edition
Copyright © 1995, 1998, 2002, 2003 by Lawrence Letham
Second edition 1998, third edition 2002, fourth edition 2003

Published simultaneously in Canada by Rocky Mountain Books, Calgary
Distributed in Europe by Cordee, 3A De Montfort St.,
Leicester LE1 7HD, Great Britain

Manufactured in Canada

Library of Congress Cataloging-in-Publication Data
A catalog record for this book is available at the Library of Congress

Table of Contents

Acknowledgements

Thank you to Natural Resources Canada for permission to use the Canadian maps on pages 81, 105 and 114. These maps are based on information taken from the National Topographic System map sheet numbers 83 E/3 Mount Robson Copyright 1980 and 83 C/3 Columbia Icefields, edition 02 Copyright 1984. Her Majesty the Queen in Right of Canada with permission of Natural Resources Canada.

The maps shown on pages 24, 29, 33, 50, 76, 95, 97, 117, 119, 122, 123, 125, 143, 144, 147, 148, 152 and 170 were produced by the U.S. Geological Survey.

The marine charts on pages 131, 133 and 135 are from the U.S. National Ocean and Atmospheric Administration.

Thank you to Martin Fox of MapTech for loaning me the Terrain Navigator Pro database and mapping program. Screen shots for the MapTech program appear in Chapters 10, 13 and 14.

Thanks to Brad Dameron of Garmin, Angela Linsey-Jackson and Lonnie Arima of Magellan, Andrea Schrug of Brunton, Steve Wegrzyn of Lowrance, and Russ Graham of Navman, Andrew Golden of Golden Public Relations and Cindy Estridge of Pharos for loaning me receivers, software, pictures and accessories produced by their respective companies. Pictures of the products they loaned me are found throughout the book.

Thanks to Larry Saunders, Jim Bodine and Dale Carpenter for loaning me their personal receivers and software to use.

Trademark List

Landranger is a trademark of Ordnance Survey of Great Britain. Street Pilot, Street Pilot III, eTrex, eTrex Legend, eTrex Venture, eTrex Summit, GPSmap 76, GPSmap 76S, Geko 101, Geko 201, GPS 12 XL, USB 35 TracPak, MetroGuide USA, GPS 12, GPS 12XL and GPS III are trademarks of Garmin International. SporTrack, SporTrack Pro, SporTrack Map, Meridian Platinum, Meridian Gold, Meridian Color, Meridian 310, Magellan 750+, Magellan 750 M, GPS 2000 XL and GPS Pioneer are trademarks of Magellan, Inc. Multi-Navigator MNS, GPS XL1000, GPS XL1000 Forest and Navimap are trademarks of Nexis-Brunton. UTM Grid Reader is a trademark of N. G. Terry. TOPO! is a trademark of Wildflower Productions. Terrain Navigator, Terrain Navigator Pro, Pocket Navigator, Outdoor Navigator, Marine Navigator, TopoScout are trademarks of MapTech. iFinder is a trademark of Lowrance Electronics. GPS Utility is a trademark of GPS Utility Limited. Navman is a trademark of Navman USA Inc. Trademarks of Navman: iCN-630, GPS 3420, e Series, m Series, p Series. Pharos is a trademark of Pharos Science and Applications, Inc. Trademarks of Pharos: Pocket GPS Navigator, Pocket GPS Portable Navigator.

1 Introduction to the Global Positioning System (GPS)

The Global Positioning System (GPS) is a satellite system used to navigate. It enables anyone on the planet who owns a GPS receiver to know where they are 24 hours a day in any kind of weather.

The GPS is a group of 24 satellites that circle the earth and beam radio signals from their positions above the earth back to the earth's surface. A GPS receiver is an electronic device that detects the radio signals from the satellites and calculates the receiver's position on the earth. GPS has affected many parts of everyday life. Shipping companies use GPS to know where their cargo is at all times and how it is progressing towards its destination. Soon, a GPS receiver will be built into every cell phone, so when you make an emergency call, your position will automatically be sent to the rescuers.

The GPS system has radically changed navigation for the outdoor adventurer, and GPS receivers keep getting better every year making it even easier to navigate in the outdoors. A recent improvement called Wide Area Augmentation System (WAAS) has increased the accuracy of GPS receivers to 3 m (9.8 ft). Improved GPS receivers have downloadable electronic maps that have the detail of the best topographic maps. Navigation has never been easier.

GPS technology is based on a group of satellites that beam radio signals back to earth.

This book will help you understand both the satellite system and GPS receivers, so you will know how to choose the receiver you need and how to use it properly.

Before describing how GPS works, it is interesting to see how hard navigation was in the 15th century. The comparison between then and now is dramatic.

A GPS receiver shows the position of each satellite and signal dtrength bars.

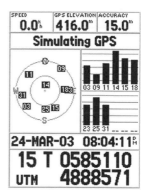

Early Navigation

The times leading up to Columbus' voyage to the New World in 1492 was an era of advances in navigation. Determining position improved from recognizing the landscape or the shore to being able to at least determine one's latitude from the sun or the stars. Latitude was relatively easy to measure because one simply had to measure the sun's arc in the sky to know their distance from the equator. The quadrant was the tool of choice for determining latitude and Columbus used one when he sailed. But there was no easy way to determine longitude except to have extensive knowledge of the stars, and most sailors did not have the neccessary mathematical skills or knowledge of the heavens. Amerigo Vespucci was the amazing exception in his day. His extensive knowledge of the stars and his mathematical abilities enabled him to determine longitude and with that ability, he made an amazing discovery.

In 1499, at the age of 48, Vespucci sailed from the Old World to the lands that Columbus discovered and claimed were India. He carried with him a book called an almanac. Almanacs were produced by astronomers and annotated the positions of the stars in the skies at exact times. Vespucci's almanac was made in Italy and was based on celestial observations and times as measured in the city of Ferrara, Italy. It just so happened on August 23, 1499 that the moon would cross Mars at exactly midnight in Ferrara. Vespucci knew the celestial occurrence was the perfect opportunity to determine his longitude. Vespucci had himself put ashore on what is today the Brazilian coast. He measured the stars to determine his exact local time then waited for the conjunction between the moon and Mars. When the moon finally crossed Mars, it was 6.5 hours after it was observed in Ferrara. Vespucci then knew that his distance from Ferrara was the distance the earth would turn in 6.5 hours. In 140 AD, Claudius Ptolemy calculated the earth's circumference to be 17,895 miles (the actual circumference is 24,900 miles). Using Ptolemy's circumference, Vespucci calculated that he was about 4,800 miles west of Ferrara. In other words, Vespucci knew his longitude in addition to his latitude. He knew where he was on the globe. Based on his calculation and his comparison of the indigenous people to the accounts he had read of the Indies, he concluded that Columbus had not discovered the Indies, but an entirely new world.

Measuring longitude was a lot easier once John Harrison produced accurate chronometers in 1761. A departing sea captain would take a chronometer that was set to the homeport time. Usually, the port time was the time in Greenwich, England. When the captain wanted to know his longitude, he would measure the local time and compare it to the time on the watch. The difference between the local time and the chronometer's time was the distance, as per the earth's circumference, from the homeport. Captain Cook carried a chronometer based on one of John Harrison's designs and found its use made it easy to measure longitude.

It is interesting to note that in the case of Vespucci or Captain Cook, if the sky were cloudy, it was impossible to determine position. Since their method of navigation was rooted in celestial observations, a cloudy day or inclement weather, meant they were out of luck.

Today, finding latitude and longitude is as simple as turning on a GPS receiver. GPS does not remove the need to do math or to know the positions of heavenly objects. In fact, the Global Positioning System is very complex, but all the complexities are hidden from the user, so that knowledge of exact position, anywhere on earth, is as easy as reading numbers from a screen or looking at the map displayed on the screen. GPS navigation is easy and reliable, even the weather does not disrupt it. GPS units work when it is cloudy, raining, snowing or when the air is filled with smoke like during a forest fire. Even though a GPS user does not need to do any thing difficult to use GPS, it is helpful to understand some of the system's intricacies.

How GPS Works

The concept of GPS was conceived in 1960 as a method to increase the accuracy of intercontinental ballistic missiles. The U.S. Air Force started developing the system and called it the Global Positioning System. In 1974, the other branches of the U.S. military joined in on the project and renamed it Navstar, but the name GPS persisted. The entire system cost $10 billion to develop and became fully operational in April 1995. Eighteen satellites is the minimum number needed to cover the whole earth, but the number of satellites in orbit fluctuates between 24 and 29 due to spares and upgrading. Tests proved the system to be accurate to about 15 m (49.2 ft). In 1998, the Wide Area Augmentation System (WAAS) was added to provide increased accuracy for use by commercial airplane navigation systems. WAAS increases accuracy to better than 3 m (9.8 ft). WAAS is explained in detail in Chapters 4 and 16. The important thing to know is that most modern receivers are WAAS enabled, which means they can receive and use the WAAS signals to increase accuracy.

The actual workings of the system are incredible. The system is divided into three parts or segments: space, ground control and users. The space segment consists of 24 satellites that orbit 20,200 km (12,552 mi) above the earth and beam radio signals towards earth at 1,227.6 MHz (called the L2 signal) and 1,575.42 MHz (called the L1 signal). The radio signals broadcast the position of each satellite in the sky and an electronic code. There are two codes sent from the satellites to earth: precision (P code) and coarse acquisition (CA code) codes. Each satellite has a highly accurate atomic clock to keep precise time and to send the codes at exactly the same time from each satellite. As will be seen, keeping accurate time is very important to the GPS.

The ground control segment is comprised of ground stations in Hawaii, Colorado, Diego Garcia, Ascension Island and Kwajalein. The ground stations track the satellites, monitor their health and make any necessary adjustments to keep the system accurate. The entire system functions under the auspices of the U.S. Department of Defense.

GPS receivers make up the user segment. It is the GPS receiver, whether it be in an airplane, a truck or in a hiker's hand that detects the radio signals from the satellites and calculates the receiver's position. The number of users does not affect the radio signals from the satellites, so every person in the world could have a receiver and the system would still operate correctly. The way the receiver uses the radio signals to calculate its position is a work of ingenuity.

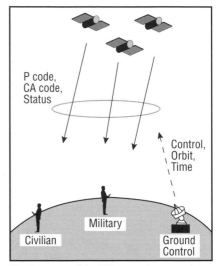

The three parts of the GPS: ground, space and user.

When a receiver is first turned on, it listens to the radio signals and extracts the satellite location information. The GPS signal broadcasts information that tells the receiver the location of each satellite in the system; even if a satellite is on the other side of the world. The receiver then listens to the radio signal to determine the exact time. It was mentioned earlier that each satellite has an atomic clock to keep very accurate time. Ground control keeps the clocks synchronized and the receiver needs to know the exact time, just like the satellites, to calculate its position. The receiver then monitors four of the satellites that are currently overhead. The design of the GPS ensures that there will be a minimum of four satellites covering any spot on the globe at all times. The receiver uses the signal from one satellite to continuously monitor and to be synchronized with the time maintained by the satellites. The receiver monitors the codes from three other satellites. The satellites broadcast the code at an exact known time and the receiver detects the exact time when the code arrives. The difference in time between when the satellite sent the code and the receiver received it is the time it took for the signal traveled from the satellite to the receiver. The speed of the satellite signals is known; therefore, the receiver can calculate the distance to the satellites. As soon as the receiver knows its distance from three celestial objects, meaning three GPS satellites, it can calculate its three dimensional position on the earth: latitude, longitude and altitude. GPS is just like navigating by the stars. If you know positions of the stars, you can mathematically calculate your position on the earth. The GPS satellites function as stars in the sky, so your receiver can calculate its position. The position the receiver calculates for latitude and longitude (horizontal position) is accurate to about 15 m (49.2 ft) without WAAS and about 3 m (9.8

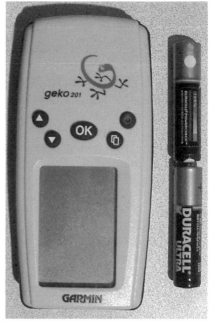

Modern receivers are small, lightweight and run off 2 AAA batteries.

ft) with WAAS. The altitude calculation (vertical position) is less accurate by about 50%, which means 22.5 m (73.8 ft) without WAAS and 4.5 m (14.8 ft) with WAAS.

Another way to try to understand how GPS works is to imagine yourself floating in a room of zero gravity. To find your exact position, you use a tape measure to determine your distance to the closest wall. You then measure the distance to another wall and finally the distance to the floor. Because the positions of the walls, ceiling and floor are known, your position is also known because you know your distance to them. GPS is much the same. The receiver knows exactly where each satellite is located even though it is moving. It uses the codes transmitted from the satellites like a tape measure to determine its distance from three satellites (the signals from the fourth satellite are still used to keep accurate time). Much like the zero gravity room, once the receiver knows its distance from three known objects, it knows where it is. The system is very complex, yet it is very simple to use.

Additional Terms and Details

You do not need to understand the GPS terms introduced in this section to be able to use a GPS receiver, but concepts explained will help you converse intelligently about the system along with understanding the meaning of some of the terms.

In the previous section, it was mentioned that the satellites beam down two different codes, so receivers can determine their position: the P code and the CA code. Both codes are strings of numbers. The P code is so long that it takes seven days to repeat itself. The CA code repeats itself every millisecond. The P code also has a higher chipping rate than the CA code, which means that it changes more frequently than the CA code. If the P and CA codes were compared to the markings on a tape measure, the P code would have millimeter (1/32 inch) marks where as the CA code would have only centimeter (1 inch) marks. The finer marks of the P code allow it to be more accurate. The bad news is that only military receivers understand the P code. Civilian receivers only have access to the CA codes. But the news really is not that bad. While military receivers are accurate under most conditions to 1 m (3.28 ft), a civilian receiver with

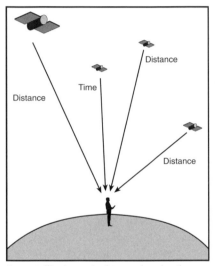

One satellite is required to synchronize time, and three more for a 3D position fix.

WAAS is accurate to 3 m (9.8 ft). Accuracy of 3 m (9.8 ft) is fabulous.

The ionosphere also plays a part in the accuracy of GPS receivers. The ionosphere is the part of the atmosphere from 150 to 900 km (93 to 559 mi.) above the earth. As a radio wave travels through the ionosphere, it slows down. As you recall, accurate timing is very important to making an accurate position calculation. The receiver calculates its distance from the satellites based on the time it takes the satellite signal to travel from the satellite to the receiver. If radio waves slow down in the ionosphere, the receiver needs to know how much the signal slowed down, so it can account for the slow down in its distance calculation. The receiver's accuracy depends on knowing how much the signal slows down in the ionosphere. There are three ways to know how much the ionosphere affects a signal. The first method is accessible only to military receivers. The P code is transmitted on both the L1 and the L2 frequencies. It is important to note that L1 and L2 are different frequencies. Radio waves of different frequencies slow down different amounts when they go through the ionosphere, which means the difference in delay between the L1 and L2 codes can be measured and used to calculate the amount of the slow down in the ionosphere. Measuring the difference in delay of the different frequencies allows military receivers to accurately compensate for the ionosphere.

Unfortunately, the CA code is transmitted on only the L1 frequency; so civilian receivers use a second method of correcting for ionospheric delay. Every civilian receiver has a model of the ionosphere built-in to its memory. The receiver uses the model to estimate the delay through the ionosphere wherever it is in the world. The ionosphere is different all over the earth and it varies throughout the day, so there are limits to the model's accuracy, which means that civilian receivers cannot fully compensate for ionosphere delay like military receivers. WAAS is the third method for correcting for ionospheric delay. WAAS uses differential GPS (DGPS) to remove the error introduced by the ionosphere. DGPS is explained in detail in Chapter 16.

You may also hear the term Selective Availability. When the GPS system was developed, the U.S. government did not want its enemies to use the system against it, so the Department of Defense deliberately degraded the accuracy of the CA codes. Under Selective Availability, the accuracy of a civilian receiver varied randomly between 15 m (49.2 ft) and 100 m (328 ft). Fortunately, Selective Availability was removed May 2, 2000 and civilian receivers without WAAS are nominally accurate to 15 m (49.2 ft).

Another type of GPS receiver is called a codeless receiver. Even though they are not useful to the mobile adventurer, they are absolutely incredible. A codeless receiver does not use the P or the CA codes—at least not directly. It uses the CA code to lock onto the satellites, and then monitors the changes in the L1 and L2 frequencies. Using a technique called interferometry, a codeless receiver can calculate its position to an accuracy of 10 mm (0.39 in.). The accuracy is incredible; unfortunately, it takes several days to make a single measurement.

2 Why Buy a GPS Receiver?

GPS receivers are popping up in more places every day. Some wrist watches have GPS receivers. Mobile phones have receivers integrated into them. Handheld GPS units are more powerful and less expensive than ever before. A GPS receiver excels at three basic tasks:

1. Leading you to a destination you choose from a map.
   The map can be:
   – A paper map.
   – The electronic map built into or downloaded into the receiver.
   – An electronic map displayed on your computer.
2. Determining your current position, which will be displayed as:
   – A coordinate you can look up on a paper map.
   – A location on the electronic map in the receiver.
3. Remembering your current position, so you can return to it later.

Everyone who travels or recreates outdoors should carry a GPS receiver. They are small, unobtrusive and can make the trip more fun. GPS receivers are effectively used in the following activities. The list is not exhaustive, but it is a good representation of a GPS receiver's usefulness.

Hiking

You need not travel off well-marked trails to appreciate a GPS receiver while hiking. Clearly, a GPS receiver is valuable for navigation in areas where there are no trails, few landmarks or close to the earth's magnetic poles where it is hard to use a compass. But even on well established trails, a GPS receiver can show you your exact position, tell you your speed, calculate when the sun will set and help you determine if you will make it to your favorite spot before dark. A GPS receiver is invaluable in poor weather or when it is hard to see your surroundings.

Hikers should look for receivers that are small, lightweight and easy on the batteries. It is nice if the receiver has built-in or downloadable maps, but always take a paper map with coordinates for backup navigation. Receivers that can connect to a computer to download waypoints before the hike or upload them after the hike are a great plus.

Most hikers will probably not have the receiver on all the time, but will take it out occasionally to see where they are. Cost-conscious hikers can get satisfactory performance out of a base model GPS receiver that does not have built-in maps or advanced features, by using the receiver only to report their current position and for tracking their progress on a paper map.

Geocaching

Geocaching is a worldwide game where one person establishes a cache and reports its location on the web. Other participants load the coordinate of the cache into their receiver then use the receiver to find the cache. By the description alone, Geocaching does not sound very difficult, but do not be fooled. Knowing something's location is vastly different from getting there. Geocaching has gained a wide following over the years. There are tens of thousands of sites established in over 160 countries. Fortunately, any receiver is sufficiently powerful to participate in geocaching because all GPS receivers are capable of leading you to any coordinate you type in.

The definitive web site for geocaching is www.geocaching.com. Go there to find a cache or to report the location of the cache you establish.

Biking

Mountain and road bikers can use more of the full power of an advanced receiver. A GPS receiver mounted on the handlebars becomes a powerful navigation tool. Bikers will want to leave their receivers on all the time, so they can continuously get speed, altitude, direction, track log and guidance information. If you mark waypoints in advance, the receiver can guide you along your desired course or tell you how to return to course after straying to explore. Most receivers can hold at least one route.

Hunting

Hunters rarely have the luxury of sticking to the trail or taking the easy route. A GPS receiver will help you get back after tracking an animal. It can help travel before the hunt by marking tree stands, locations of heavy animal traffic or good camping spots before setting out.

Look for a receiver that has good battery life even when the screen's backlight is on for maneuvering in the dark. You need the same features as a hiker, but your trail will be much less predictable.

Kayaking and Canoeing

Sea and river kayaking and canoeing is a lot like hiking on well-marked trails; you do not need the receiver to keep you from getting lost, but it does provide lots of information otherwise not readily available. Kayakers and canoers can use GPS receivers much like bikers to monitor speed, direction, total distance paddled, route traversed, proximity to landmarks or exact position when there are no landmarks. On open water, a receiver helps the paddler paddle directly from one point to the next; thereby, saving energy and time. It also helps locate that hard-to-find put-in or take-out. Some receivers allow the user to mark areas to avoid and the receiver beeps when you get too close. Others have an anchor drag warning beep.

Be sure to get mounting gear to attach it to your craft. Long battery life is important. If the unit is not waterproof, put it in a clear, waterproof bag before mounting. Downloadable electronic maps are available for much of the U.S. shores.

Fishing

GPS units have been developed specifically with fishermen in mind. Although this book does not describe GPS/sonar combination units, fishermen will find handheld GPS receivers invaluable for marking the best biting spots on stream, lake or ocean. A receiver with a track log helps you troll more effectively because you can see where you have been and where you need to go for complete coverage. A receiver can also keep you in one location, so you do not unnoticeably drift away from where the fish are biting. A GPS receiver helps ice fishermen find the shack regardless of the weather. Most receivers are waterproof to some extent. Some receiver manufacturers produce downloadable waypoints of hot fishing spots.

Ski Mountaineering

Ski mountaineers use GPS receivers much like hikers until whiteout conditions occur. When the cloud rolls in, the GPS receiver is invaluable because it works regardless of the weather. Ski mountaineers should mark waypoints in good weather or in advance from a map, so when the nasty conditions occur, the receiver can steer you from one waypoint to the next. If you are in an area where WAAS is supported, use it because accuracy while groping your way back is vital. You need a receiver with a backlit screen and take lots of extra batteries, so the receiver can be used continuously during the trip through the clouds. Even though a receiver will be immensely helpful, still take standard precautions like placing wands and roping up on crevassed glaciers. Using a GPS receiver to maneuver back to base camp when the cloud is down is described in Chapter 7.

Sailing

Today, one should not go out on the open seas without a GPS receiver. Knowing your current position is vital when plying a ship through sea lanes, around reefs and by islands. Although many manufacturers offer powerful and expensive GPS units for mounting on a ship, a full feature handheld unit can meet all your navigation needs. Be sure to buy a unit that supports nautical units and the map datum you will be using. Upper-end receivers support at least a hundred datums. If you want to use the receiver on the bridge, get a unit that supports an external antenna and get the antenna. If there is a cigarette lighter on the bridge, get a power cable for the receiver, so you can have continuous operation without using a lot of batteries. If you sail in areas where electronic maps are available, get a receiver that supports downloadable electronic maps.

Car Travel by Road

Road travelers are the biggest beneficiaries of GPS technology, map databases and powerful GPS receivers. GPS receivers specifically designed for vehicles have detailed map databases and large screens to display the downloaded maps. You can specify an address and the receiver calculates a route to get you there. It shows your current location on the map on the screen, reports your speed, direction, where to turn and how much longer the trip will take. More advanced models actually talk to tell you each turn and maneuver required to arrive at your destination. The map databases also include lists of amenities like hotels, gas stations, restaurants and sightseeing attractions along the way. Most receivers mount on the dashboard and receive the satellite signals through the windshield, but it is advisable to get an external antenna, so the passenger or someone in the back seat can hold the receiver without disrupting the reception of the satellite signals. Most GPS receivers designed for vehicles come with a cigarette lighter power adapter, so you can save on batteries.

Professional Uses

Professional uses of GPS increase in number every day fuelled by the greater accuracy provided by WAAS. Anyone whose work requires high resolution surveying or accurate position recording should consider using GPS technology. Forestry personnel, prospectors, oil and gas exploration crews, geologists, archaeologists, biologists, etc., can all benefit from using a GPS receiver.

Search and Rescue

GPS is invaluable to search and rescue units. Receivers track what has been searched and direct teams to where they need to be to continue the search. The receivers used by search and rescue teams should have a track log that can be downloaded into the computer used to coordinate the search. Downloading track logs or waypoints marked in the field by searches allows the search coordinator to track progress and provide a record of how the search was conducted.

Mushroom Hunting

GPS technology is a boon to dedicated mushroom hunters. Use any type of receiver to mark the best morel beds and the most productive areas for successful harvesting year after year.

3 Backing up your GPS Receiver

You bought a GPS receiver. It's the latest model. You have already found five geocaches close to your neighborhood, so you know how to use it. Now it is time for a backcountry adventure. You load a map of the area into your receiver, you download waypoints along the trail and you pack extra batteries. Are you really ready to go? You are close, but not quite ready because you need to have a backup navigation plan.

Although GPS receivers are rugged and the electronics probably will not fail while you are out on the trail, conditions can occur that render your receiver useless. The most obvious failure mode is physically breaking or losing your receiver. If your entire navigation plan depends on the receiver and you have no back-up navigation equipment, you could be in trouble if you lose or break your receiver.

Another possible scenario, where the receiver does not function as planned, is if the terrain blocks the satellite signals and makes it so your receiver cannot lock onto enough satellites to get a position fix. Remember, a receiver must be able to detect at least four satellites to provide an accurate position fix. Generally, the type of things that might interfere with satellite reception are really rugged terrain, very heavy foliage or traveling at the bottom of deep canyons. Fortunately, terrain is not an insurmountable factor because the satellites are always moving. If your receiver cannot detect enough satellites one moment, it will be able to see different satellites a short time later.

Anyone taking a trip should take backup equipment and methods of navigation. One could argue that taking a second GPS receiver is sufficient backup equipment. That argument has its merits, but the best backup navigation plan is one that relies on entirely different technology, even if it is primitive compared to a GPS receiver.

Everyone going on a trip through less familiar territory should always carry at least a map and compass and should know how to use them. Other useful backup navigation tools are a pedometer, a watch, an altimeter and a notebook. On most trips, the GPS receiver will perform flawlessly and there will be no need for backup equipment, but do not stake your life, or even the discomfort of spending an unexpected night outdoors, on a single method of navigation.

Beginning navigators, who know how to use only a GPS receiver, can use their receiver to learn how to use a map and compass. With practice, you can acquire enough skill to adequately navigate with map and compass. Those who wander far from the beaten path or in featureless areas may have to learn celestial navigation as their backup. For most adventurers, a compass, a watch, a notebook and a map, as described below, are all that are needed for backup navigation.

A Travel Notebook for Backup Navigation

A small notebook, pencil and watch are invaluable tools to the navigator. They can help you get back just in case your receiver malfunctions. Use the notebook to make any notes that will help you remember the course you traveled. Make a quick sketch of the intersections and show which fork you took, record the number of tributaries you passed in your canoe and note the kilometer or mile marker numbers closest to where you turned off the main highway. Keep track of your position relative to any prominent landmarks. It is important to record the time as you make notes, so you can estimate the distance you have traveled. The farther you travel from the established trail, the more descriptive and important your notes become, but as a bare minimum on any trip over a new trail, regardless of how easy you think it may be, keep track of the time between intersections to help you more closely estimate how long it will take to return. Also record from your receiver some navigation information such as the bearing traveled, but be sure you have the receiver set to magnetic bearings so you can use them with your compass if necessary.

If your receiver stops working, there is no reason to panic because the information in your notebook will guide you back to your starting point. All you need to do is traverse the route in reverse and watch for the landmarks you noted. If your notes include direction of travel, calculate the reverse direction and use your compass to walk it. Refer to Chapter 17 to understand math with bearings and how to calculate the opposite direction of a bearing. Continue making notes on the return trip to be able to verify that you are on the right course and how long you have been en route. Use your compass to take bearings, and make note of the surrounding landmarks to ensure that they are the same ones

1. *6:00 am Break camp. Rough road to here.*
Followed faint trail.
2. *6:42 am At Smith Ravine Spring.*
Spring is damp, but not running.
Continue down dry wash.
Ridge on left.
3. *7:50 am Pass between two small peaks.*
Road on map visible, very rough.
4. *8:05 am Followed visible valley.*
Not very steep. Peak rises ahead.
5. *8:35 am Easy ascent. Good View.*

Sample fieldbook entry.

you saw on the way in. A notebook is vital in the field because it helps you accurately remember even in stressful moments.

A notebook is important even when your receiver is working just fine. A receiver stores the coordinates of a location and some receivers allow you to store a descriptive message, but it is not long enough to describe why you marked the spot. You could record a camping location and even type in the message "GREAT CAMPING SPOT," but three days later you will not remember why it was so great. If you make an entry in your notebook, you will remember the wood close by for fires and the overhanging rock that provided shelter from the rain. Your notes do not have to be extensive, but if you record what you see and feel, your notebook will bring back enjoyable memories for years to come.

Using a Map for Backup Navigation

Unless you are in an area you know really well, your navigation gear should include a paper map. While the receiver is working, the map is used to track your position and the notebook records time and information about significant waypoints as explained above. You can also write down bearings between waypoints if you want to, but that information is available from the map. If you do put bearings in the notebook, be sure to indicate if they reference magnetic or true north. Maps are not always up-to-date, so add any important features directly to the map because they may be important if you have to return without the aid of your receiver. The map becomes the visual record of your journey while the notebook provides any memory jog-

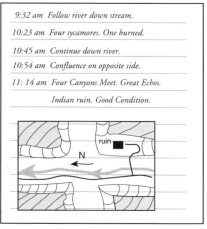

9:32 am Follow river down stream.

10:23 am Four sycamores. One burned.

10:45 am Continue down river.

10:54 am Confluence on opposite side.

11:14 am Four Canyons Meet. Great Echos.

Indian ruin. Good Condition.

If a picture helps you remember your route, draw it in your field notebook

ging information that will help you recognize your location. Once again, the notebook is a valuable aid in recognizing the return route.

If your receiver stops working, you can use the map, notebook, compass and watch to get back to your starting point. The direction of the return route is measured from the map and sighted with the compass. Do not forget to account for declination, which is discussed in Chapter 4. Using a map and compass to track your journey is much better than the notebook alone because the map provides more information than could ever be written in a notebook. Refer to Chapter 11 for an example of how to deal with poor reception or a broken receiver.

Why GPS Receivers Stop Working

Of all the reasons why a receiver might stop working, one thing you do not have to worry about is the termination of the coarse acquisition (CA) code broadcast from the satellites. The U.S. Department of Defense could turn off the CA code, but they will not do it for two reasons. First, military receivers use the CA code to synchronize with the precision (P) code. After a military receiver locks with the CA code, it waits for the appropriate moment to switch over to the P code. Without the CA code, military receivers could not synchronize with the P code, so they would not work. The second reason is because lots of military units use civilian receivers. At least they did in the first Gulf War. In fact, during that war, the satellite orbits where changed to provide better coverage in the Middle East. Another factor that virtually guarantees that the CA codes will not be turned off is that GPS is highly integrated into civilian activities. GPS is so pervasive that denying civilians access to the system would cause great hardship.

It is unlikely your receiver will just stop working under normal conditions. Today's receivers use integrated circuits and advanced assembly techniques, so they are as reliable as your computer, television or stereo and most are designed to sustain the rigors of outdoor use.

It is the everyday occurrences that will leave you without your receiver: dead batteries, losing it, getting it wet or dropping it. Whatever the cause, one minute you know where you are and the next, you are wondering if you will ever find your way back again—that is if you are unprepared and do not have a backup plan. Go prepared with backup skills, take lots of batteries and do not worry.

4 About GPS Receivers

There are a lot of affordable GPS receivers on the market with features to meet every need. The importance of a feature depends on how you intend to use the receiver, so the features and capabilities of handheld GPS receivers are described here to help you select the receiver most suited to your needs. Fortunately even receivers in the lower price ranges are loaded with features, so you probably will not need to make a choice between a feature and your pocketbook.

This chapter first describes features common to all receivers such as antenna sensitivity, accuracy with and without WAAS, map datum and grids. Not all receivers have all the features described in the chapter, but you should be able to find one that has the combination of features you need.

Important GPS terms are defined and explained in this section, but if you happen to forget one or two, check the Glossary for a quick review. The phone numbers and web pages for GPS manufacturers are listed on page 204.

Receivers vary in size from one that fits in the palm of the hand (right) to slightly larger.

Antennas

The antenna picks up the signals sent from the satellites. It is the most important part of a receiver because if the antenna cannot detect the satellites' signals, there is no way the receiver can even begin to calculate your position. Fortunately, the antennas manufactured in today's receivers perform well in the field and you should not have any problems. However, if you plan to travel in remote areas where the satellite coverage can be limited to the four satellites guaranteed by the system's design, you may want to purchase an external antenna and use it because they are usually more sensitive and perform better than most built-in antennas.

Handheld receivers are equipped with one of two types of antennas:

Quadrifilar Helix

- Rectangular in shape, usually external to the receiver
- Swivel it to point to the sky for best reception

Patch (Microstrip)

- Smaller than Quadrifilar helix
- Usually internal to the receiver
- Hold parallel to the sky for best reception

Either antenna type will perform properly and adequately in the field. There is one advantage of the quadrifilar over the microstrip antenna. Many quadrifilar antennas can be detached from the GPS receiver, which means they can easily become external antennas by connecting a coaxial cable between the antenna and the receiver. This

simple and inexpensive adaptation allows the antenna to be placed outside a vehicle for better reception while the receiver remains inside directing the driver. The cable should not be too long or the signal that reaches the receiver is seriously attenuated and rendered useless.

While the microstrip's internal construction protects it from harm, if you do not exercise care the quadrifilar antenna can get caught on a branch or other object and be damaged.

External Antennas

External antennas are separate from the receiver and connect to the receiver by a cable. External antennas are a must if the receiver is used inside an enclosed area like a boat's cabin, a cockpit or inside a vehicle. An antenna must have an unimpeded view of the sky to pick up the satellite signals. Although it is possible for a receiver on a car's dash to detect the signals through

Garmin external antenna.

the windshield, it is hard for the driver to see the receiver's screen at the same time. It is far better to place an external antenna on the roof of the vehicle and mount the receiver, so it is accessible and usable to the driver.

External antennas are waterproof and can be used in any type of weather. They mount either magnetically or with suction cups. Another reason why you may need an external antenna to use a receiver in a car is because some windshields have a transparent layer of metal sandwiched between the layers of glass. Although you can see out, the metal blocks the satellite signals, so the receiver does not work.

Usually, external antennas are more sensitive than the internal antennas, so they can detect and lock onto satellites when the internal antenna may not work. Not all receivers are designed for external antennas. If you think you may want to use an external antenna sometime in the future, be sure to buy a model that accepts one. Usually, the manufacturer is the only source of an external antenna for a given receiver. An "active" external antenna amplifies the signal before sending it to the receiver to compensate for any attenuation or signal loss though the wire. If you have the choice, it is best to have an active antenna.

Accuracy

The first question everybody asks is: "How accurate is my receiver?" The short answer is:

Without WAAS

- 15 m ((49.2 ft.) horizontal accuracy
- 19 m (62.3 ft.) vertical

With WAAS

- 3 m ((9.8 ft.) horizontal accuracy
- 6 m (19.7 ft.) vertical

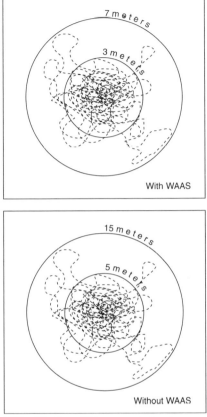

With WAAS

Without WAAS

95% of the time, GPS accuracy is 5 meters without WAAS and 3 meters with WAAS.

If you were to stand in a fixed location for several hours or days and make a plot of the positions your receiver reported, it would look like the figures opposite. Even though you did not move, the receiver reports different positions because factors like the atmosphere and satellite geometry affect the accuracy of the receiver. The accuracy is generally stated as how close it will get you to the center of the circle 95% of the time. For a receiver that uses WAAS, it is accurate to 3 m (9.8 ft.) 95% of the time and is never less accurate than 7 meters.

A geographical representation of accuracy is shown in the figure on the next page. The map is the U.S. Geological Survey map of Mirror Lake, Utah (scale 1:24,000) with grid lines 1000 m (3281 ft.) apart. Three circles, one near Scout Lake, a second southwest of Camp Steiner and the third on the road, are each 30 m (98.4 ft.) in diameter, which means the edge of the circle is 15 m (49.2 ft.) from the center point. If you wanted to go to one of these points and you did not have a WAAS enabled receiver, you would get somewhere within the circle. The dot just north of Tadpole Lake and the building (circled) just south-southwest of Scout Lake are approximately 6 m (19.7 ft.) in diameter or 3 m (9.8 ft.) from the center point. A WAAS enabled receiver would take you somewhere inside these points.

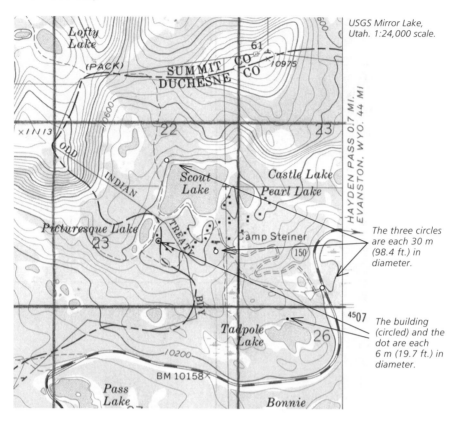

USGS Mirror Lake, Utah. 1:24,000 scale.

The three circles are each 30 m (98.4 ft.) in diameter.

The building (circled) and the dot are each 6 m (19.7 ft.) in diameter.

Looking at the map above it is clear that WAAS makes navigation quite accurate. So, you need to understand what WAAS is all about.

What is WAAS?

WAAS stands for Wide Area Augmentation System. It is a collection of ground stations that use differential GPS techniques (see Chapter 16) to calculate the amount of error in the GPS signals. Information to correct for the error in the GPS signals is then transmitted to one of two WAAS satellites stationed over the equator, which in turn transmit the correction information to GPS receivers. When using WAAS, a GPS receiver calculates its position using the GPS satellites' signals then it uses information from one of the WAAS satellites to correct its calculated position. WAAS does not help the receiver determine its location, but it provides data to help the receiver refine its position calculation once it is established. WAAS was developed to increase GPS accuracy for airport landing systems.

WAAS coverage is not global. It is designed to cover the Continental U.S. and Alaska. Hawaii will also be covered in the future. Agreements between the U.S. and Canadian governments will also provide coverage to Canada in the future. If you travel where there is WAAS coverage, be sure to use it because it increases accuracy significantly. If you travel in an area not covered by WAAS, be sure to turn this feature off on your receiver. If the receiver picks up WAAS signals in an area that WAAS does not cover, the receiver's accuracy can be adversely affected and result in accuracy worse than 15 m (49.2 ft.).

WAAS Coverage

WAAS coverage is available inside the circle.

FAA documents state that accuracy using WAAS is 7 m (23 ft.), yet GPS receiver manufacturers claim that the accuracy is 3 m (9.8 ft.). As mentioned above, accuracy is generally specified as accuracy over a percent of time. WAAS makes a receiver accurate to 3 m (9.8 ft.) 95% of the time. The remaining 5% of the time, the receiver is accurate to 7 m (23 ft.). In other words, if you use your receiver to go to the same location 100 times, 95 times you will arrive within 3 m (9.8 ft.) of the destination. The other five times, you will arrive within 7 m (23 ft.) of the destination.

Just as a side note, the FAA plans to deploy an additional system called Local Area Augmentation System (LAAS) that will make GPS even more accurate. LAAS will be implemented and used primarily around airports. Each installation will cover an area with a 30 - 50 km (20 - 30 mi) radius. It will require a separate VHF radio receiver to pick up the signals broadcast from a LAAS ground station. It probably will not be adopted for civilian receivers because it will require extra equipment and will cost more. If it is adopted by GPS manufacturers for commercial receivers, it most likely will be an add-on feature much like differential GPS has been in the past. The FAA web page at http://gps.faa.gov/index.htm provides detailed information about WAAS and LAAS.

More on Accuracy

That simple answer given above to the question about a receiver's accuracy is generally true in areas of optimal satellite coverage. If you travel in remote areas of the world or simply want or understand more about receiver accuracy, you need to know that accuracy depends on:

- Ionospheric interference
- Satellite geometry
- Reflected or multipath signals

Ionospheric Interference

The concept of ionospheric interference was described in Chapter 1. Basically, the signals from the satellites slow down in the ionosphere. If the receiver knows how much the signals slowed down, it can accurately calculate its position. If it does not know how much the signals were affected by the ionosphere, its position calculation will be inaccurate. Military receivers cope with ionospheric distortion by transmitting the satellite signals on dual frequencies. Civilian receivers rely on mathematical models of the ionosphere. Ionospheric delay accounts for 5 to 10 m (16.4 to 32.8 ft.) of error of the total 15 m accuracy. WAAS corrects for a lot of the error introduce by the ionosphere.

Satellite Geometry

Satellite geometry, also known as satellite constellation, refers to the satellites' positions in the sky relative to your position. The most ideal geometry is to have one satellite directly overhead and the other three evenly spaced around the horizon.

The amount of error introduced by satellite geometry is called Dilution of Precision (DOP). There are several components of DOP: vertical, horizontal, time, position and geometric. The receiver calculates each component for each combination of four satellites it has in view and uses the signals from the four satellites that provide the lowest position DOP (PDOP) number. Poor geometry increases the receiver's position error by hundreds of meters. Normal PDOP values of between 1 and 3 will provide 15 m (49.2 ft.) accuracy. PDOP values between 4 and 6 can cause inaccuracies ranging from tens of meters to hundreds of meters. If the PDOP value is greater than 6, the receiver will not lock, resulting in what is known as an outage. An outage can also occur if the terrain blocks the satellites capable of providing the lowest PDOP. There is not much you can do when poor satellite geometry results a large position error or an outage except wait for the constellation to change. Fortunately, the satellites are constantly moving, so an outage that is not caused by terrain should last only a few minutes.

There are two factors that can help minimize outages. The first is the receiver's mask angle and the second is antenna sensitivity. If you plan to use your receiver in remote areas of the world, where satellite coverage is not as great as in heavily populated areas, you want a receiver that has a low mask angle and a very sensitive antenna.

Receivers are designed to improve accuracy by ignoring satellites that are close to the horizon. The mask angle refers to the number of degrees above the horizon a satellite must be before it is used to calculate a position. Most receivers have a mask angle between 5°

and 10°. The larger the mask angle, the more a receiver is affected by outages because it stops using satellites near the horizon sooner than a receiver with a lower mask angle. The constellation that provides the lowest PDOP is when one satellite is directly overhead and the others are evenly spread across the horizon. If a receiver has a high mask angle, it will prematurely ignore the satellites providing the best constellation.

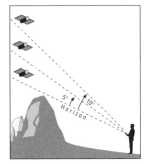

Mask angle.

The GPS constellation is designed to provide coverage from at least four satellites at all times and at all places in the world. If your travels take you to a place where the minimum number of satellites is available most of the time, you will want the best antenna money can buy. An antenna that cannot detect all four available satellites could mean that you will either suffer from outages or your receiver will work only in the two-dimensional mode, which can be highly inaccurate.

Most receivers do not display DOP values, but they do provide an Estimated Position Error (EPE) that is an indication of the PDOP. EPE shows the amount of error due to the satellite geometry. As you navigate, occasionally look at the EPE to see if you need to cope with more error than the accuracy stated above.

EPE reading from a receiver shown as accuracy.

Reflected or Multipath Signals

In ideal conditions, the GPS satellite signals go directly from the satellite to the receiver. If the signal is reflected by something in the terrain, it can have more than one path to the receiver's antenna. A reflected signal is called a multipath signal. In the figure, the signal from a satellite arrives at the receiver both directly and as a reflected signal from a nearby cliff. Presently, only survey grade (which means very expensive and usually heavy) receivers can detect and eliminate reflected signals. A consumer grade receiver cannot tell the difference between the direct and reflected signal. If it uses the reflected signal to make a position calculation, it will be wrong. As you use your

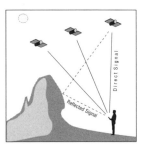

Reflected or multipath signal.

receiver, be conscious of your surroundings and avoid terrain that may result in a multipath error.

Altitude Accuracy

The altitude provided by a GPS receiver is not as accurate as the horizontal position; however, WAAS can provide an altitude measurement accurate to 6 m (19.7 ft.), which is pretty good. If you need more accurate altitude measurements, you should buy a good altimeter. Higher-end GPS receivers have built-in electronic altimeters and even track your altitude over time. Some wrist watches also have electronic altimeters.

Some GPS receivers track altitude over time.

Accuracy in the 2D Mode

Position readings in the two-dimensional (2D) mode are less accurate than readings in the three-dimensional (3D) mode. A receiver must lock onto four satellites to be able to get a 3D position fix. A receiver uses the four satellites to determine its position as follows:

- One satellite's signal: synchronize receiver with satellite's atomic clock
- Three satellites' signals: find 3D position

If the receiver locks onto only three satellites, it still has to use the signal from one of them to synchronize the time, so only two are left to calculate the position. The 2D position calculation omits the altitude. The horizontal position accuracy in the 2D mode ranges from 150 m to 1524 m (492 to 5000 ft.). A receiver working in the 2D mode may not even get you to within sight of your destination. You may have to lean a little more heavily on your manual navigation skills in such a situation, which is yet another reason to keep your manual skills practiced.

Map Datum

Maps are drawn so every point is a known distance and height from a standard reference point called a datum. A grid is a series of lines on a map that helps you describe a location in reference to the datum point. A map can have several grids, but only one datum. Before you buy a receiver, make sure it supports the datum for the maps you want to use.

Most receivers support the two most common datum for North America: North American Datum 1927 (NAD 27) and World Geodetic System 1984 (WGS 84). If you travel or live internationally, you may need different datum, so know which datum you need before you buy.

Before entering any coordinate into your receiver, be absolutely sure you set the receiver to the correct datum or there will be an error in the coordinate. Before GPS, each country independently chose their own datum, then made their maps, so the same location can have different coordinates on different countries' maps. Imagine you want to fly over Humphreys Peak, which is the highest point in the state of Arizona, USA. From a USGS topographical map you measure the coordinate:

Humphreys Peak N 35° 20' 48", W 111° 40' 41"

When you enter the coordinate into the receiver, you do not notice that the Reunion datum is selected instead of NAD 27. When you get in your plane, the receiver directs you to the point you stored, but it is not even close to the peak. When you check the receiver and change the datum to NAD 27, the coordinate you stored changes to:

Humphreys Peak N 35° 19' 55.8", W 111° 40' 21"

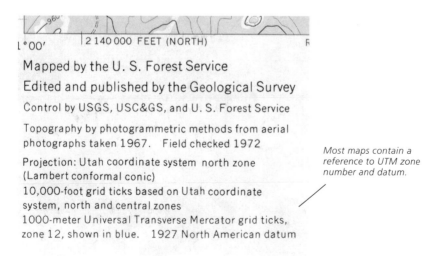

L°00'   2 140 000 FEET (NORTH)   R

Mapped by the U. S. Forest Service

Edited and published by the Geological Survey

Control by USGS, USC&GS, and U. S. Forest Service

Topography by photogrammetric methods from aerial photographs taken 1967. Field checked 1972

Projection: Utah coordinate system north zone (Lambert conformal conic)

10,000-foot grid ticks based on Utah coordinate system, north and central zones

1000-meter Universal Transverse Mercator grid ticks, zone 12, shown in blue. 1927 North American datum

Most maps contain a reference to UTM zone number and datum.

Entering the coordinate with the wrong datum resulted in a position error of 1.7 km (1.05 mi.). The Reunion datum is an extreme example because the differences between some datum are small, but all the same, it is something you do not want to have happen. Be sure to set the datum correctly before you enter any coordinates.

Selecting a map datum.

There are hundreds of map datum. Some examples are:

WGS 84: World Geodetic System 1984
A datum for the whole world as defined by GPS

NAD 27: North American Datum 1927 Continental
Used at present by older Canadian and U.S. maps

NAD 83: North American Datum 1983
Used by new Canadian maps and U.S. maps in the future

OSGB: Ordnance Survey Great Britain
Great Britain, Scotland, Isle of Man.... Note there is also a grid by the same name—do not get confused

Geodetic Datum 1949
New Zealand

Built-in Maps

Many receivers have what is called a base map stored permanently in the receiver's memory. A base map usually has all major highways and some major surface streets for a given area, like the U.S., Canada, Europe, South Africa or Australia. Some receivers can use a computer to load more detailed maps into memory for display on the receiver's screen. Downloadable maps usually contain minor streets, a street address look up function and points of interest. Even topographical maps are available to be downloaded into a receiver.

Display of built-in map.

Currently, downloadable topographical maps are the 1:100,000 scale variety. Electronic maps and map databases are discussed in Chapter 13.

Memory

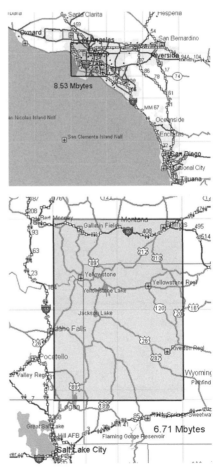

With the advent of downloadable maps, the amount of memory built into the receiver or the size of the memory sticks that can be inserted into the receiver becomes an important issue. The answer to the question of how much memory is really needed in a receiver depends on how you use it. If you travel over a limited area or a group of limited areas, you need just enough memory to cover the area.

The amount of memory required for a specific area depends on the information available for the area. For example, the amount of memory required to store the road maps from Garmin's MetroGuide USA for Los Angeles (top) is 8.53 Mbytes and the area surrounding Yellowstone (bottom) is 6.71 Mega Bytes (MB). Note, however, that

8.53 MB of map data covers only 497 square miles of the LA area, while 6.71 MB of map data covers 53,075 square miles around Yellowstone. If you know what type of area you will traverse before you buy your receiver, you can purchase a receiver with enough memory to cover your needs. If you are not limited on funds, get a receiver with as much memory as possible or if you have access to a portable computer while you travel, you can transfer maps to your receiver as you need them.

Some manufacturers have taken another approach to downloadable maps by storing the map data on removable memory sticks like those used in digital cameras.

Tiny MMC memory cards provide a flexible way to manage downloadable maps.

If the receiver you want uses memory to store downloadable map information, you either buy one big memory stick and store all the maps you need or buy several and store different areas on different sticks. Memory sticks are definitely the best approach to storing downloadable data, but do not let that be a factor in purchasing your receiver unless you cover a wide area in your travels and anticipate frequently changing the downloadable information that is available to the receiver.

Coordinate Grids

A coordinate grid is a pattern of lines drawn on a map to uniquely describe every point. The grid identifies a place on a map using a combination of letters and numbers called coordinates. Different locations cannot have the same coordinate. GPS receivers display coordinates, so once a receiver locks onto the satellite signals, the letters and numbers displayed on its screen are your position on the map. It is important to buy a receiver that supports the grid used by the maps you have available.

At about this moment, you are probably thinking you can skip this section and all other sections that deal with using paper maps and reading coordinates. After all, you have probably seen a high-end receiver loaded with detailed maps. You happen to know that you can pick a position from the map shown on the GPS receiver screen and can store it as a waypoint without ever knowing its coordinate. That knowledge leads you to conclude that grids are unimportant because

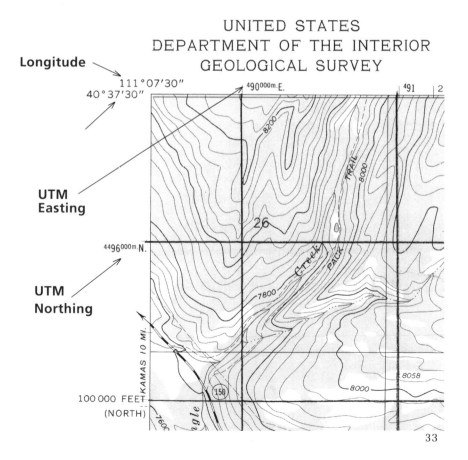

UNITED STATES
DEPARTMENT OF THE INTERIOR
GEOLOGICAL SURVEY

Longitude

UTM Easting

UTM Northing

you can do everything on either a computer or on the receiver without ever looking at a coordinate. You are partially correct, but the part in which you are in error makes grids even more important.

Excellent electronics maps of road systems can be found for many parts of the world. If you travel the roads and highways in the U.S., Canada, Europe, South Africa or Australia, you may be able to navigate without ever knowing a thing about coordinates; however, the second you want to go off-road or to an area that does not have electronic maps, you will have to rely on paper maps, which require you to understand coordinates. It will be a long time before every square inch of any country, including the U.S., is entirely covered by electronic maps with sufficient detail to completely eliminate paper maps, so until that distant day arrives learn to fully use your GPS receiver by understanding and knowing how to use coordinate grids.

Do not buy a receiver that does not support the Universal Transverse Mercator (UTM) and latitude/longitude grids because together they cover most of the paper maps used in the world. You will always be able to find a map that has one or the other. Some receivers only support UTM and latitude/longitude, which is enough for most users. However, there are grids that pertain to specific countries, such as the Ordnance Survey grid of Great Britain. If you plan to use your receiver in Great Britain, it is best if your receiver supports the Ordnance Survey grid because it is used in a wide variety of British maps.

Some Popular Grids

- Universal Transverse Mercator (UTM)
- Latitude/Longitude
- British Grid (OSGB)
- Military Grid Reference System (MGRS)
- Maidenhead
- Universal Polar Stereographic (UPS)

Selecting a coordinate grid.

The most common grids, UTM and latitude/longitude, are thoroughly explained and demonstrated in Chapters 5 through 9. The other grids are briefly described here with more information found in Chapter 15.

OSGB

Used by the excellent Ordnance Survey maps of Great Britain.

MGRS
The grid used by the U.S. military. It is based on the UTM grid, but it replaces some numbers with letters. Until the advent of electronic map databases, the MGRS was not readily accessible to civilians. Now anyone can print a custom map with the MGRS grid. See Chapter 15 for more information.

Maidenhead
The grid system used by amateur radio operators.

UPS
Developed to cover the Arctic and Antarctic regions. Similar to the UTM grid.

All receivers can switch from one grid to another and some receivers display two coordinate grids on the screen simultaneously. Other receivers make it easy to switch between coordinate grids. If you know you will need to use coordinates in two different grids, buy a receiver that allows conversion between the two to be done with as few button presses as possible.

Below are some examples of the coordinates of the places using different grids. Note the British Grid is valid only in Great Britain.

Calgary, Alberta, Canada
11 U 703421m.E. 5662738m.N.	UTM
N 51° 4' 55.2", W 114° 5' 44.6"	lat/long
11 U QG 03421 62738	MGRS
DO21WB	Maidenhead

New York, New York, USA
18 T 583926m.E. 4507327m.N.	UTM
N 40° 42' 50.9", W 74° 0' 23.0"	lat/long
18 T WA 83926 07287	MGRS
FN20XR	Maidenhead

Harrogate, England
SE 31000 55000	OSGB
30 U 596556m.E. 5982957m.N.	UTM
N 53° 59' 23.7", W 1° 31' 37.7"	lat/long
18 T WE 96556 83957	MGRS
IO93FX	Maidenhead

Subsequent chapters explain more about the grids and will help you decide which one is best for your navigation needs.

Computer Interface

Computers are now an important piece of navigation hardware. Most receivers, even entry-evel ones, are capable of interfacing with a computer. You want a receiver that can interface with a computer, so you can at least transfer waypoints marked in the field to your computer for long-term storage. The programs that run on a computer and are useful with GPS receivers are discussed in Chapter 13. A computer can make waypoint selection and entry before the trip much faster and more efficient than typing in one letter or number at a time using the receiver alone.

Most receivers are capable of two-way communication with the computer, which means that information can be transferred from the computer to the receiver and vice-versa. Do not buy a receiver that can do only one-way communication. You do not need to worry about the computer not speaking the receiver's language because there are standards set by the National Maritime Electronics Association (NMEA) that are adhered to by both software and hardware manufacturers. The current NMEA protocol is 183 version 3.0. Be sure your receiver supports it.

Most manufacturers also have a proprietary interface language. Many programs support the proprietary languages in addition to the NMEA protocol. The types of interface languages found on receivers are:

NMEA 183 version 3.0

As described above, NMEA is an industry standard language. Some receivers also support earlier versions like 2.0 or 1.5. Any version is capable of working with other types of equipment. The NMEA protocol is used to communicate with moving maps, chart plotters, automatic pilots and other types of equipment that need position information to do their job.

Selecting NMEA for the computer interface.

RTCM SC-104

RTCM SC-104 is the industry standard format for Differential GPS (DGPS) correction information. Chapter 16 fully describes DGPS. DGPS is not WAAS. If you want to have access to DGPS, you must have a receiver that understands

RTCM. Most users will not want to use DGPS because it requires additional equipment, which costs more money. Furthermore, WAAS is more convenient and does not cost any more than buying a WAAS capable receiver.

Text
Some receivers are capable of sending out text (ASCII) characters. Text output is not governed by an industry standard, so the information provided will depend on the manufacturer.

Channels

All modern receivers have 12 parallel channels. Parallel channels allow a receiver to simultaneously track up to 12 satellites. The term "parallel channels" means that all the satellites are simultaneously and continuously tracked.

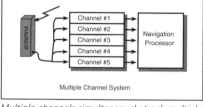

Multiple Channel System

The satellite signals enter the antenna then go to the channels. One channel locks onto the first satellite in view; another channel locks on to the next satellite and so forth until every satellite visible in the sky is assigned a channel. The channel continuously tracks its as-

Multiple channels simultaneously track multiple satellites.

signed satellite as long as it is in view. The information from the channels goes to the navigation processor where the satellites that provide the best DOP values are used to calculate position. Rarely does any area on the globe get coverage from more than 10 satellites, so 12 parallel channels is as good as you will ever need.

Having parallel channels ensures that the navigation processor always has the most accurate information available to make a position calculation. If you are walking past a big tree in the woods that suddenly blocks a satellite, the navigation processor immediately grabs the information from the next best satellite to calculate your position.

Waypoints or Landmarks

The coordinate of a location is called either a waypoint or a landmark. Receivers require not only the letters and numbers of the coordinate of a location, but also a name.

Navigation with a GPS receiver starts when you enter the waypoint of where you want to go into the receiver's memory. You can do this either by typing in the coordinate and name on the receiver's keypad or by selecting a point on the receiver's built-in map or by selecting a point from a map on your computer and then transferring the waypoint to your receiver. The receiver determines your present position, calculates the distance and direction to the destination waypoint and directs you to it. Because waypoints are the foundation of GPS navigation, you want your receiver to be able to store as many as possible. As an indication of how many you may need, it takes 10 to 15 waypoints to adequately describe a 16 km (10 mi) trail that is traveled on foot. It takes between 45 and 65 waypoints to plan a trip by road between San Diego, California and Portland, Maine. The least expensive receivers on the market can store at least 250 waypoints, so you will be able to store the waypoints for several trips in the receiver. The number of waypoints a receiver can hold need never be a limitation because you can store all your waypoints on your computer and transfer only the waypoints you need to the receiver for your planned trip. Computer programs that work with receivers are discussed in Chapter 13.

Each waypoint consists of a coordinate and a name, but unfortunately most receivers limit the name to between 6 and 10 characters. A few receivers allow names as long as 20 characters. You want the name to remind you of the location, so you may have to be creative. Many receivers also allow for a short descriptive line

Waypoint with its coordinates and elevation.

Automatically generated name.

List of waypoint names.

or a symbol to help remind you of the location. If the receiver provides an appropriate symbol, use it. If you use a computer to manage your waypoints, fill in the descriptive line using the computer since typing on a computer keyboard is much faster than entering letters on the receiver's key pad. The description will help you remember where you marked the location.

Available symbols.

If you do not want to type in a name, most receivers will automatically generate one for you. For example, the first time you mark a waypoint, the receiver will call it 001 or LMK001. The next waypoint will be called 002 or LMK002 and so forth. If you need to mark a lot of waypoints quickly, let the receiver name them. You can either rename them later or keep the receiver generated names since their position on the receiver's built-in map will show you their location.

The coordinates of a waypoint can be either your current location or any location in the world that you enter into your receiver. The power of a GPS receiver lies in the fact that you can get a coordinate from any source, whether it be a paper or electronic map or a geocache web page, and your receiver can calculate the distance from your current position to that waypoint and show you how to get there.

All waypoint information—the name, the coordinate and the comment—are stored in the receiver's memory. Providing the batteries are not dead, information in memory is not lost when the receiver is turned off. Some receivers have small backup batteries or use flash memory (same type of memory as in cell phones), so the information stored in the receiver's memory is not lost even when the batteries are completely removed.

Waypoint Manipulation

Because waypoints are fundamental to GPS navigation, your receiver must make it convenient and easy to enter, retrieve and modify them. If the receiver makes you press a lot of buttons to do something, you will not enjoy using it and it will collect dust on the shelf. You do not want a receiver that requires you to type in every letter of a waypoint's name before its coordinate is displayed on the screen or its location is shown on the built-in map. Listed below are the convenient ways many receivers allow the user to access the waypoints stored in memory:

- Alphabetized list of waypoint names with prompting
- Waypoints listed by proximity to present position
- Selection of a waypoint displayed on the receiver's built-in map

Imagine you have the following waypoint names stored in your receiver: BAYOU, BINSTER, BOAT, BUOY, CAMP, DOCK 4, HJFALL, REEL, RIVER, ROCK, RUFF, TOWER, TUCMAC, TZEGI and VORTEX. Here is how the typical receiver will access these waypoints using the methods listed above.

The letter "B" is displayed after "A" during serial selection.

Alphabetized List

If you know the name of the waypoint you want to review, the fastest way to get to it may be to simply access the receiver's waypoint screen and type in its name. Once you have entered the name, the waypoint's coordinate and other information appears on the screen. Typing in an entire name could be time consuming (see the section on Data Entry, page 74), but a feature called prompting makes it go faster. Prompting enables the receiver to jump to the appropriate waypoint by typing only the first few letters of the name. Good receivers use prompting whenever you need to specify a waypoint's name, like when selecting waypoints to form a route. Receivers are not like a typewriter where you can randomly select any letter of the alphabet. There are two common ways receivers enable the user to access the alphabet: sequentially and by a table. Sequential selection means you

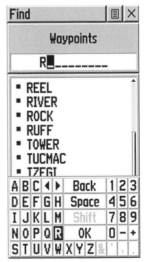

The alphabet table allows quick access to any letter.

start at the beginning of the alphabet and cycle sequentially through the letters until it displays the correct one. For example, you press a button and the receiver displays the letter "A." You press it again to increment the letter to "B," then again to go to "C," etc., until you reach the letter you want. Cycling serially through the letters is slow, so the receiver speeds up the search for waypoints by prompting with the names of waypoints already stored in memory.

For example, if you want to see the waypoint ROCK, you cycle through the alphabet for the first letter. When you select "B" as the first letter, the receiver shows the name "BAYOU" on the screen. It is prompting you to select the first waypoint stored in its memory that starts with a "B." If you want to see the BAYOU waypoint, you would press enter, but as you are looking for ROCK, you press the button again, the first letter changes to "C", at which point the receiver prompts you with the waypoint named CAMP. When you press the button again, the first letter advances to "D" and the receiver displays the waypoint DOCK 4. You press the button until the alphabet advances to the letter "R" and the ROCK waypoint is visible on the receiver's screen. Now you can press the button that allows you to select the ROCK waypoint from the alphabetized list. You could also sequentially search for the second letter in the same manner. When you press the button to advance the second letter, the prompting jumps directly to "I" for the second letter and displays the waypoint RIVER. The letter "O" appears when the second letter is advanced again and the waypoint ROCK is displayed. At this point you press enter and the waypoint ROCK is selected and displayed at the top of the alphabetized list.

Manufacturers have developed an even faster way to access an alphabetized list of waypoints by combining prompting with an alphabet table. As shown in the figure, an alphabet table displays the alphabet in rows and columns. To select any letter, you press the up, down, left or right buttons to move between the rows and columns of the table. Selecting any letter from the table can be done with at most six keystrokes, so the table is much more efficient than the sequential method. The receiver also prompts with stored waypoints, so when you select "R," the receiver displays the waypoints that start with "R." You can either select the second letter to be "O" or you can just select ROCK from the alphabetized list. An alphabetized list combined with an alphabet table provides fast, easy access to stored waypoints.

Nearest Waypoint List

If you have a receiver with lots of memory to store waypoints, a list sorted by nearness to your present position helps separate the waypoints of totally different areas. If you are in a certain location, you are probably only interested in the waypoints local to your position. A nearest waypoint list is great for those receivers capable of storing several hundred waypoints and saves you the time of hunting through a large alphabetized list because if a waypoint is close, it appears at the top of the list. Selecting a waypoint from the nearest waypoint list is

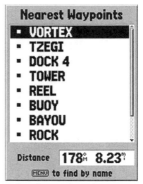

A list of waypoints close to your current position.

fast and simple because all you have to do is use the buttons, usually the up and down ones, to highlight the waypoint you want.

Waypoint from Built-in Map

A receiver that has a map screen also allows waypoints to be selected from the map. The figure shows your position at the black triangle near the waypoint TZEGI. Any waypoint shown on the map can be selected by moving the cursor, in this case the light colored arrow, to the waypoint of interest. When the cursor touches the waypoint, you can select the waypoint and its information is displayed on the screen. It is possible to select any waypoint stored in memory from the receiver's map, but it is most conveniently used as a visual version of the nearest waypoint list.

Selecting the ROCK waypoint with the cursor.

Proximity or Dangerous Waypoint List

Some receivers provide a proximity list to warn you when you approach hazardous locations. The proximity list can be used to keep your boat out of shallow waters or you out of a sinkhole. The coordinate of the dangerous areas must be entered as a waypoint, and then placed on the proximity list. The list allows you to specify how close you can get to the object before the receiver sounds a warning. If the receiver's units were set to statute miles, the list shown would

Setting proximity alarms.

keep you 1.5 mi. (2.41 km) from DOCK, 1.75 mi. (2.82 km) from BUOY, 2 mi. (3.22 km) from ROCK and 5 mi. (8 km) from VORTEX.

Goto Function

The true power and utility of a GPS receiver is summed up in the word Goto. All receivers are capable of leading you to a place you have specified using either a Goto or route capability. You simply select a previously stored waypoint or select a location from the built-in map then tell the receiver to guide you there. The power to Goto any place is fundamental to GPS navigation.

You must veer to the left to get to the Bayou waypoint.

The receiver guides you to your destination using a steering screen. There are several different versions of a steering screen, many of which are described below, but they all fundamentally do the same thing: they point the direction you need to go to get from your present position to the waypoint you selected. The receiver not only points the way, but it tells you if you are off course, your speed, when you should arrive and other useful information that is described in the section titled Navigational Statistics.

Goto the REEL waypoint by selecting Goto.

Some receivers have a separate Goto button while others activate Goto by finding a waypoint from an alphabetized list then activating the receiver to go to the selected waypoint. Once you select your destination, follow the receiver's directions display on the steering screen. Receivers lead you in a straight line directly to the waypoint. If the best route is not direct or if the direct route has obstacles, you may be better off using the Route function. The Route function allows you to specify several intermediate points between you and the final destination, which can be used to steer around difficult or dangerous terrain.

Some GPS receivers with downloadable electronic road maps can plan a route from your current position to the final destination that follows the road system, but such an advanced feature is currently available only on high-end receivers. All computer programs that handle road maps can plan a route that stays to the roads. After the computer plans the route, it can be transferred to the receiver.

Routes

A route is a list of waypoints that describe the path you will travel. It is like the Goto function, but it leads you to many points sequentially instead of to just a single destination. The Route function is important because it enables the receiver to guide you from the first point in the route to each successive waypoint until you reach your final destination. It is similar to the Goto function because it allows you to specify where you want to go, but it is more powerful because you can also choose the path you take. The Route function is also more automatic than Goto. When you reach one waypoint on a route, the receiver automatically switches to guide you to the next waypoint without you touching a single button. With the Goto function, you must manually select the next waypoint before you start out again. Most receivers, except for the most basic, have at least one route. The Route function should have the following capabilities:

Route	
VORTEX-TUCMAC	
Waypoint	◀ Distance ▶
VORTEX	0.00ᶠ
DOCK 4	26.8ᵐ
REEL	41.1ᵐ
TOWER	68.4ᵐ
BAYOU	77.6ᵐ
CAMP	91.9ᵐ
TUCMAC	112ᵐ
Total	**112ᵐ**

The route starts at VORTEX and ends at TUCMAC. Its total length is 112 miles.

- 10 - 20 waypoints per route if used by foot.
- 30 - 50 waypoints per route if used in a car using software to route the trip.
- Automatic route reversal.
- Display navigation information between points.

All the waypoints for a route must be stored in memory or must be part of the base map. Placing the waypoints on the route list in the order they are to be traveled forms the route. Forming a route is easy because the receiver prompts you for waypoint names already stored in memory or allows you to select waypoints from the built-in map.

If you use a software program on your PC to form a route, say for a road trip, the route cannot have more waypoints than the receiver allows per route. If you plan a long trip of over 100 waypoints, but your receiver only allows 50 waypoints per route, the route will be truncated when transferred from the computer to the receiver. Long journeys must be broken up into routes that fit into the number of waypoints the receiver allows. A receiver that has more than one route allows a long journey to be spread over many routes. Do not worry too much about the waypoint limit because 50 waypoints will cover a trip of between 2,500 and 3,000 miles on the road.

Once the route is developed, you activate it and the receiver points the way you should go to get from the first point in the route to the second. It uses the same steering displays as the Goto function. When you arrive at the second waypoint, the receiver informs you of your arrival and immediately points the way to the third waypoint. The process continues from one waypoint to the next until you reach your destination.

Automatic route reversal means the receiver makes the destination the starting point, the starting point the destination, and puts all the intervening waypoints in the correct reverse order. Automatic route reversal means you do not have to manually form another route when you want to return. Once the route is reversed and activated, the receiver once again points the way from one waypoint to the next until you arrive at your original starting point.

Most receivers calculate and display the bearing and distance between the waypoints that form the route to give you a rough idea of the trip's total length. Planning a road trip using routes on a computer is even better than on the receiver because the computer asks for your driving speed then calculates the total time to make the trip.

Compass

Do not throw your compass away, unless of course you purchase a receiver with a built-in electronic compass. A receiver, without a built-in compass, is not at all like a compass. All receivers report the direction of your travel as long as you are moving because it calculates the direction between your current location and where you were a few seconds ago. If you stand still, the receiver can no longer calculate your direction of travel. If you stand still with a receiver and turn slowly around in a circle, the bearing will not change because you are standing still and the receiver does not have a previous location to use to calculate your direction of movement.

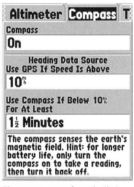

The setup page for a built-in electronic compass.

A compass uses the earth's magnetic field to measure your bearing relative to the magnetic pole. If you hold a compass and turn around slowly, the compass needle will move to continually point to the magnetic pole. An electronic compass built into a receiver also works off the earth's magnetic field, so it can determine your direction even when you are not moving. The great thing about a built-in compass is that the

Leveling bubble on a Brunton receiver.

receiver can automatically compensate for declination, something you have to do manually with a stand-alone compass.

Most receivers allow the user to specify when the electronic compass reading will be used over the receiver's calculated bearing. If you are going faster than you can walk and are generally in motion, the bearing calculated by the receiver will be accurate. On foot, you will probably want to always depend on the electronic compass.

The receiver has to be held level to the ground when using the electronic compass much like an ordinary compass should be held level when used. Receivers either provide a bubble level or a message on the screen to help you level the receiver when using the compass.

Altimeter

Not only have electronic compasses been incorporated into some receivers, but altimeters have been too. Although a receiver can use the satellite signals to calculate altitude, a built-in altimeter can provide a more accurate altitude reading especially in areas not covered by WAAS.

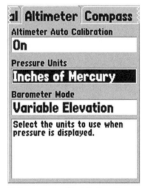

Setup screen for electronic altimeter.

Built-in altimeters work off of barometric pressure, which is the pressure of the surrounding air or atmospheric pressure. The atmospheric pressure at sea level is greater than the atmospheric pressure on top of Mount Everest because as you climb higher, the amount of air above you decreases. An altimeter must know its starting elevation then, as the barometric pressure varies, it converts the change in pressure into a change in altitude. Unfortunately, changes in weather bring changes in atmospheric pressure, which affects the accuracy of a barometric altimeter. The units of atmospheric pressure are inches of mercury, millibars or kilo-Pascal. Be sure the receiver supports the unit of atmospheric pressure used in your area.

Most receivers allow the altimeter to be used in one of two ways:

• User calibrated
• Automatically calibrated

In the user calibrated mode, the user must specify the initial elevation or atmospheric pressure and must periodically, depending on local changes in weather, recalibrate the altimeter. Automatic calibration uses the elevation reading calculated by the receiver based on the GPS satellite signals as the starting elevation. The electronic altimeter is automatically recalibrated periodically using the current GPS calculated elevation. If the weather is not changing and you have an accurate starting elevation, the altimeter elevation will be more accurate than the elevation calculated by the receiver, so set the receiver to the user-calibrated mode. If the weather is changing or you do not know your starting elevation, use the automatic calibration mode. The automatic calibration mode enables the altimeter to theoretically improve altitude readings at least until the altitude is automatically recalibrated.

User calibration of an electronic altimeter.

Bearing (Azimuth)

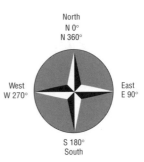

The term bearing as it is used in this book is more correctly called an azimuth. Look for both terms in the Glossary if you want a deeper explanation, but for most people the word bearing is simply the compass direction between your present position and your destination. The bearings of the cardinal compass directions (East, West, North and South) are shown in the figure. If you travel due east, your bearing is 90°.

The bearings between the waypoints MINE,

CAMP and TOWN are:

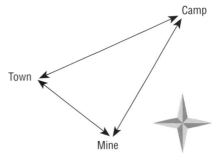

Start	Destination	Bearing
MINE	CAMP	30°
MINE	TOWN	295°
CAMP	TOWN	240°
CAMP	MINE	210°
TOWN	CAMP	60°
TOWN	MINE	115°

Receivers can report the bearing between your present position and any other waypoint or between any two waypoints. Bearings can be

relative to the north pole or the magnetic pole, so be sure you know which one is selected before you use a bearing. If the magnetic mode is set, the receiver automatically compensates for declination any place in the world. The difference between true and magnetic bearings is explained in the section titled North Settings.

Working with bearings, even calculating a return bearing, is easy, but if you need a refresher turn to Chapter 17. Mils are explained in the same chapter.

North Settings

There is more than one north and when the receiver reports a bearing, you need to know which north it references. Do not buy a receiver that does not provide both true north and magnetic north modes. A receiver may provide some or all of the following modes:

- True north
- Magnetic north
- User-defined north
- Grid north

Before explaining the various types of north, it is important to understand the difference between the two most important: true north and magnetic north. True north is the direction of the north pole, which is on the axis through the center of the earth. Magnetic north points to the magnetic pole, which is southeast of the north pole on Bathurst Island in northern Canada. Magnetic declination is the difference, in degrees or mils, between the north pole and the magnetic pole from your position. The figure below shows declination throughout the

Magnetic declination in North America.

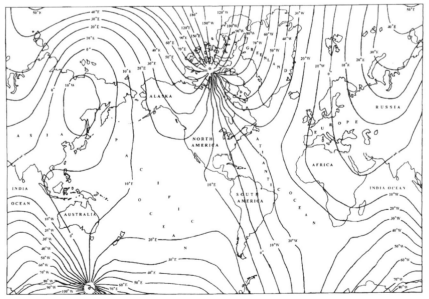

Magnetic declination around the world.

49

world, while the one above it shows how declination is measured. It is expressed as an east or west direction depending on whether the magnetic pole is to the right or left of your present position.

To manually convert a true north bearing (map bearing) to a magnetic bearing (compass bearing), remember the following phrase:

East is Least, West is Best

This means you subtract east declinations and add west declinations. Here are some examples:

- Map bearing = 50°, Declination = East 12°
  Compass bearing = 50° - 12° = 38°

- Map bearing = 276°, Declination = West 17°
  Compass bearing = 276° + 17° = 293°

In **true north** mode the receiver shows all bearings referenced to the north pole. When the receiver reports a direction of 0°, you are headed directly for the north pole. A bearing of 180° takes you directly to the south pole. Maps are oriented to the north pole, so set the receiver to the true north mode when using it with a map. A bearing is converted to magnetic simply by switching the receiver to the magnetic north mode or by using the manual conversion described above. Many receivers already know the declination for any area in the world and perform the conversion correctly.

Magnetic north mode references all bearings to the magnetic pole. When the receiver is set to the magnetic north mode, all bearings directly relate to the compass. If the receiver says the bearing to the destination is 109°, set your compass to 109 if you want to use it to get to your destination. To convert a magnetic bearing to a true north bearing, simply change the receiver mode to true north or use the inverse of the manual procedure described above.

UTM GRID AND 1974 MAGNETIC NORTH
DECLINATION AT CENTER OF SHEET

User-defined north allows the user, not the receiver, to specify declination.

Grid north is the direction to which the grid on the map is aligned. In most situations, grid north is the same as true north. Some receivers allow you to enter the grid declination if you are using a map that does not have the grid aligned with true north. Usually the difference between grid north and true north is so small that it can be ignored without consequence.

Declination diagram from a USGS 7.5 minute series map. The magnetic declination is E 13.5°. The difference between true north and grid north is W 14 mils.

Data Formats

Make sure you buy a receiver that displays speed, distance and bearings in the units you prefer to use. Most receivers report speed, distance, altitude, CrossTrack Error, etc., in three different formats:

- Metric: kilometer, kilometers/hour
- Nautical: nautical mile, knots
- Statute: mile, miles/hour

It is important that a receiver be able to display information in all the above formats because each coordinate system is best suited to a particular unit. For example, UTM, UPS, MGRS and OSGB are best used with metric units as their grid is a kilometer-based grid. The latitude/longitude grid is based on nautical units, which is used on many marine charts, but most adventurers in the U.S. prefer to use statute units. Some receivers are capable of reporting speed, distance and altitude all in different units, which means you can mix and match units.

Compass	Time	Units	L:
Elevation		Vertical Speed	
Feet		**ft/min**	
Distance and Speed			
Statute			
Depth		Temperature	
Feet		**Fahrenheit**	
Direction Display			
Numeric Degrees			
Speed Filter			
Auto			

Selecting the units displayed by the receiver.

Some receivers provide two units for bearings:

- Degrees
- Mils

Bearings are more widely stated in degrees, but it is nice to have a receiver that can do the conversion between the two. Refer to Chapter 17 for more information on degrees and mils.

If the receiver has a built-in altimeter, the unit selected for elevation is the unit that must be used for calibrating the altimeter.

Navigational Statistics

If you are on foot, it is nice to know the direction and distance to your destination, but information like speed, estimated time of arrival and other navigational statistics are not as important because you are moving slowly and you probably do not keep the receiver on all the time. The situation changes when you are in a car, boat, plane, snowmobile or any other vehicle where you can leave the receiver on all the time and get a constant stream of data telling you where you are and when you will get to your destination. Your specific use of a GPS receiver will determine which navigational statistics are useful to you. Read the descriptions below of each statistic, and then look for the receiver that has the ones you need.

Navigational statistics that are available on most GPS receivers:

- Distance
- Speed
- Desired course
- Current course
- CrossTrack Error (XTE) aka Course Deviation Indicator (CDI)
- Course to Steer (CTS) aka To Course
- Turn (TRN)
- Estimated Time en Route (ETE)
- Estimated Time of Arrival (ETA)
- Time
- Glide ratio

Distance

Receivers provide a variety of distance measurements. Except for the distance reported by the trip odometer, all distances are straight-line distances between two points. Receivers can provide:

Distance to destination The distance from your current position to the final destination of the active route or to the active Goto waypoint.

Distance to next waypoint in route The distance from your current position to the next waypoint of the active route.

Trip odometer The actual distance you have traveled just as it would be measure by a car odometer.

Maximum and minimum elevation The highest and lowest elevations reached.

Total ascent and descent Total ascent is the change in vertical position while traveling up. Total descent is the change in vertical position while traveling down.

Although some receivers can measure the vertical distance traveled, they do not have the ability to include the vertical distance in the calculation of the distance between two points, so the distance to the next waypoint is calculated as though your current position and the next waypoint were at the same altitude.

The distances are given in the units you select: statute, metric or nautical. Many receivers allow the altitude to be displayed in units different from the horizontal distances between waypoints. Altitude can be displayed in feet or meters. The rate of ascent or descent can be given in feet/minute, meters/minute or meters/second.

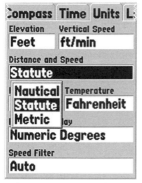

Selecting statute units for horizontal distance and speed.

Speed

A receiver measures the time and distance between the point where you are now and the point where you were a second ago then divides the distance by the time to get the speed. Some of the speed statistics reported by receivers are listed below. The meaning of each type of speed is described to help you know what a speed reading really means.

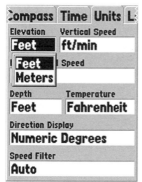

Selecting feet for the elevation unit.

- Speed (SOG).
- Velocity Made Good (VMG).
- Average Speed.
- Average Moving Speed.
- Maximum Speed.
- Vertical Speed.
- Vertical Speed to Destination.
- Average Ascent and Descent.
- Maximum Ascent and Descent.

One type of speed not listed above is the "standing still" speed. Changes in the satellite signals and positions can make a receiver report that you are moving even when you are standing still. Most receivers use averaging algorithms to eliminate false speed reports at no or low speeds; however, if you use an older receiver, just ignore random fluctuations in the reported speed when you are not moving.

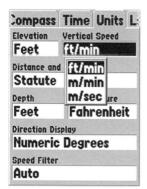

Selecting feet/minute for the vertical speed unit.

Receivers have upper speed limits, so if you plan to use your receiver at really high speeds, be sure it will work at such speeds before you buy it. All speeds are reported in the units you select: miles per hour, kilometers per hour or knots.

Speed, also known as **Speed Over Ground** (SOG) or ground speed, is just like the speed given by the speedometer in a car; it measures how fast you are going at that very moment. Speed does not take into consideration if you are on course; it is a measurement of your velocity regardless of direction.

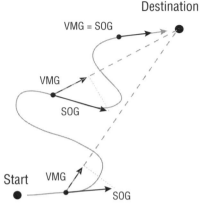

Velocity Made Good Velocity Made Good (VMG) is the speed at which you approach your destination. VMG takes into account your present course and your destina-

Relationship between SOG and VMG.

tion. If you are directly on course, VMG is the same value as SOG, but if you stray from course, VMG decreases and is less than SOG. The figure shows how VMG and SOG relate.

Unlike speed, Velocity Made Good does not always have to be positive. If you are moving directly away from your destination, your VMG will be the same as your speed, but it will be negative.

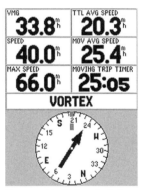

The speed is 40.0 mph, but the VMG is less by virtue of being off-course.

Average Speed Average speed is not the same as Speed Over Ground (SOG). SOG is your speed at any given second. If one second you go 25 mph (40.2 k/h), the SOG shows 25 mph. If a second later you go 50 mph (80.5 k/h), the SOG instantaneously changes to 50 mph. Average speed divides the distance you go by the amount of time it took. Suppose you have driven your car for a long time and the average speed is 25 mph. When you suddenly accelerate to 50 mph, the average speed does not immediately change, but slowly starts to rise. After you have traveled 50 mph for as long as you traveled at 25 mph, the average speed is only 37.5 mph (60.4 k/h).

Average speed tells you how fast you really go in heavy traffic. If your trip starts out at 60 mph, the average speed is 60 mph. When you hit a

traffic jam, your speed goes to zero and the clock keeps counting, so the average speed decreases the longer you do not move.

Average Moving Speed The average moving speed is you average speed excluding the time you stand still. Like the average speed, average moving speed is calculated by dividing the distance traveled by the time it took to travel, only when your speed goes to zero, the clock stops until you get moving again. If your travel is stop and go, the average moving speed will always be greater than the average speed.

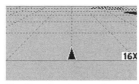

Heading directly away from the destination results in a VMG that is the exact opposite of the speed.

Maximum Speed Maximum speed is exactly what it says—the fastest speed traveled during the trip.

Vertical Speed Vertical speed is your instantaneous speed measured for up and down movements only. If you are traveling up a hill, you are moving horizontally, or forward, at some speed and also up the hill at some other speed. The vertical speed ignores the amount you move forward and measures only the amount you change in altitude. If you stop moving or hit a flat section on the trail, the vertical speed instantaneously goes to zero.

The trip computer shows average speed, moving speed and maximum speed among other statistics.

Vertical Speed to Destination Vertical speed to destination is analogous to velocity made good (VMG). It is a measure of your speed in the vertical direction with respect to the altitude of the destination.

Average Ascent and Descent Much like average speed, the average ascent or descent is the distance of vertical movement divided by the amount of time to make the movement. It is the average rate of your change in altitude. Even though you are moving forward while moving upward, the average ascent or descent is the vertical part of your movement only.

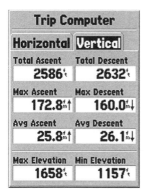

Ascent and descent statistics for a trip.

Maximum Ascent and Descent Just like it sounds, maximum ascent or descent is the maximum rate of a vertical change in position.

Direction Indicators

All directions calculated by a receiver can be expressed as a bearing. Some receivers can be set up to express direction in terms of the cardinal letters N, NE, E, SE, S, SW, W and NW. Even though you may be more comfortable using cardinal letters, understanding and using numerical bearings is much more accurate. For example, the numerical bearings for northeast, due east and southeast are 45°, 90° and 135° respectively. If the receiver reports your direction as E for East, your direction of travel can be anywhere between 68° and 112°. You cannot tell if you are closer to 68° or to 112°. A numerical bearing leaves no room for doubt. If the receiver reports your direction as 90°, you are definitely going East. Bearings are described earlier in this chapter.

All receivers provide at least the direction you are going and the direction you should be going to get to your destination. The bearing you are currently going has names like:

- Course Made Good (CMG)
- Track (TRK)
- Heading (HDG)
- Bearing

The bearing you should take to get to your destination may be called:

- Course Made Good (CMG)
- Track (TRK)

Deviation from Route Indicators

Whenever your current direction of travel does not match the direction of the Goto destination or the next waypoint in the active route, you are off course. A GPS receiver can tell you not only how far off course you are, but it can tell you what to do to get back on the correct track.

Statistics like CrossTrack Error (XTE) and Course Deviation Indicator (CDI) tell you how far off the intended course you have strayed. Receivers also provide information like Course to Steer and Turn, which tell you how to get back onto the correct course. Each statistic is described in detail below.

CrossTrack Error (XTE) measures the distance between you and the direct line between the point you started from and your intended destination. XTE is most helpful to pilots of boats or planes because they have the freedom of movement to maintain a direct course. Those on foot or in off-road vehicles usually have to go around many obstacles, so they are less concerned about how far they are from the direct course and more concerned about the bearing from their present position to the destination. However, there may be times when you can maintain a straight line and XTE is useful. If you use your receiver on roads, XTE is meaningless because you are confined to the roads. A good map screen is more useful.

The solid line in the figure is the direct course between Start and Destination. The receiver always tries to steer you on a straight line between two points. When you stray, the XTE is the perpendicular distance between the straight line and your current position. The dashed lines up the page show the CrossTrack Error to the right and left of the direct course. As you can see, XTE varies with your distance from the straight line. The point of maximum XTE is indicated for each major excursion. Whenever you are on the direct line, XTE is zero. Those points of no XTE are circled.

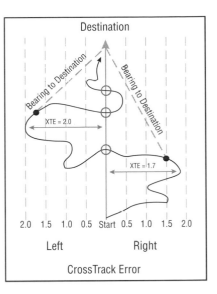

You can always return to the direct course by traveling the opposite direction of the XTE until XTE is zero. For example, if you have strayed to the left, you would travel to the right to return to the direct course. XTE is measured in the units you select for the receiver: kilometers, miles or nautical miles.

Regardless of how far off track you may be, the bearing reported by the receiver is the direction from your present position to the destination. If you get really far off track and it does not make sense to return to the straight line course, simply follow the bearing that leads from your current position to the destination.

A **Course Deviation Indicator (CDI)** graphically shows the amount and direction of CrossTrack Error. CDI displays are best utilized when your mode of travel permits you to go directly from the starting point to the destination without any diversions. In a situation where you are required to travel a certain corridor, like a pilot who must fly a designated flight path, CDI is very useful.

The CDI screen based on dots can be combined with an arrow that points the direction to the destination along with numbers for bearing, distance, heading and speed.

The two most common ways for showing XTE are indicated in the figure. In both cases, the display shows if you are off course to the right or the left and how far you are off course. The tolerance for the CDI can be set from very small to large. It is measured in the units you select, so it can be kilometers, miles or nautical miles. Most receivers have CDI ranges from 0.25 (kilometers, miles or nautical miles) to 5. If you want to stay

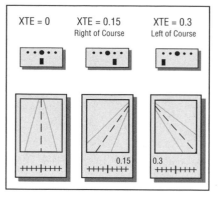

strictly on the direct course, set the CDI limit to the smallest setting. A large CDI limit allows you to stray far from course and still be able to see how to get back.

The CDI display in the upper part of the figure uses dots to indicate the direction and amount of deviation. The small rectangle under the dots represents your position and the center dot is the direct line course. The dots to the right and left of center indicate the amount you are off course. In this example each dot is 0.15 units. When the rectangle is under the center dot, you are directly on the straight line course and your XTE is zero. If the rectangle moves under the first dot right of center, as shown in the figure, you are to the right of the direct course by 0.15 units. If the rectangle moves left of center, you have strayed to the left of the course. In the figure, the rectangle is below the second dot to the left, which means you are 0.3 units off course to the left.

Headed directly to the destination, but off course to the left by 7.08 feet.

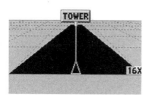

Headed directly to the destination, but off course to the right by 0.13 mile.

The second CDI display is combined with what looks like a highway. The center line represents the straight line between the two points. The highway provides more information than the other display because it not only reports deviation from course, but also shows the direction from your present position to the destination. The upper display shows only XTE. However, many receivers combine the upper

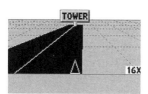

display with a small arrow that indicates direction to the destination. The tick marks under the display indicate the amount of XTE. The center mark represents your present position in relation to the straight line course. As you stray to the right of the course, the tick mark moves to the right of the center line as shown in the figure. The XTE is also shown numerically and in this case it is 0.15 and 0.3 units.

It is instructive to see what each display looks like along a path that is not even close to the straight line. The figure top right shows the displays at four different points. Note that the highway always indicates the direction you need to turn to head directly from your present position to the destination. At point P4, you gave up trying to get back to the straight course and simply turned until the highway pointed straight up and you traveled directly to the destination. At P4, there is still a CrossTrack Error, but as you are headed directly for the destination, the highway is pointing straight up.

Course to Steer
When you happen to stray from the straight line course between two points, the receiver calculates the most efficient direction to return to course. Each brand of receiver determines the course to steer (CTS) bearing differently, but it is usually a compromise between returning to the straight line course and heading directly to the destination. CTS is often indicated as the amount and direction you should turn to return to your course. The figure bottom right indicates that you must Turn 19° right to return to course.

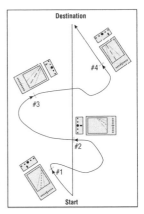

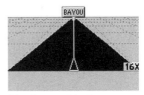

Directly on straight-line course to BAYOU, so CTS (Turn) is zero.

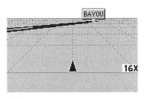

Off the straight-line course. Must turn 19° right to return to course.

Estimated Times

Most receivers provide the estimated time of arrival (ETA) and the estimated time en route (ETE), which is also known as time to go (TTG). ETA is the time of day when you will arrive at the destination, like 10:15 am. ETE or TTG tells you how much longer you must travel before arriving at the destination and is measured in minutes or hours. ETA and ETE are accurate only if you are headed directly to the destination. Both estimated times are calculated using velocity made good (VMG), which was explained earlier. The ETA and ETE are useful only in situations where you can travel directly, like in a boat or plane, to the waypoint without any detours. When a receiver is used on foot or in a car, it is possible to break up the trip into a route with lots of waypoints, so that the route between each waypoint is direct, but the ETA or ETE applies only between your current position and the next waypoint in the route. Some receivers report the estimated time to the next waypoint in a route, along with the time to the route's final destination. High-end receivers with electronic road maps and auto-routing capability can also accurately report ETA and ETE.

The time to the next waypoint in the route is 8 minutes. The time to the final waypoint in the route is 2 hours and 54 minutes.

Timers

Receivers report a variety of times as navigation statistics.

Trip time Also known as elapsed time, the trip timer measures time from the last time it was reset. The trip timer is used to calculate average speed because it continues counting time regardless of whether you are moving or not.

Time moving Time moving is the amount of time your speed is not zero. When you come to a stop, the time moving timer stops counting. The time moving is used to calculate the average moving speed, so the average moving speed is your average speed, but only when you were moving. It ignores the time you were not

The Total Time, shown on the right, is the same as the elapsed time.

moving, so the average moving speed is generally high than the average speed.

Time not moving The time not moving timer counts only when you are standing still. It represents the time you sit motionless on the freeway during your daily commute. If the time on the time moving and the time not moving timers are added, they should equal the trip time timer.

The Stopped Time timer tracks the time you do not move..

Time of day All receivers provide the time of day. The GPS satellites keep what is known as GPS time, but receivers can convert GPS time to Universal Time Coordinated (UTC). UTC is a 24-hour time measurement referenced to Greenwich, England. Greenwich is the location of zero degrees longitude. Midnight in Greenwich is zero hour on the UTC clock. The time in any area of the world is an offset from the UTC clock. Most receivers allow the user to specify their time zone as Eastern, Central, Mountain, etc., so the receiver can convert UTC to local time. Some receivers do not ask for the local time zone, but allow the user to enter the difference between UTC and local time. For example, the offset for Arizona is -7:00 hours.

Selecting the Hawaii time zone for the local time.

Glide Ratio

Some receiver provide a navigational statistic know as the glide ratio or the glide ratio to the destination. The glide ratio relates to simultaneous horizontal and vertical movement. It is the ratio of horizontal movement to vertical movement. Although the glide ratio will be reported if you are moving on the ground over terrain that changes in altitude, it is most useful if you are in some type of aircraft such as a plane or a glider.

Navigation Screens

Position Screen

The position screen is the screen where the receiver reports the coordinate of your current position. Many of the newer GPS receivers have user programmable screens, which means that you can customize most screens to provide the information you think is most important. If you are using your receiver with a paper map, you will need to set up your receiver to display your current coordinate. Most receivers have at least one page that permanently displays your position in the coordinate system you select. Some receivers allow you to display your position in two different coordinate systems like UTM and latitude/longitude.

Steering Screens

Steering screens are useful only when the receiver is activated in the

Goto or Route mode. It points the way to the active Goto waypoint or to the next waypoint in a route. There are two main types of steering screens.

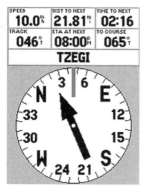

The **Compass Navigation Screen** is also known as a pointer because it points the direction you should go. It is the best screen to use when you have to go around obstacles and cannot travel directly to the destination. Hikers find it especially useful when used in conjunction with a compass. The arrow always points the direction from your current position to the destination waypoint. Following the arrow leads you to where you want to go.

Go to the left to the TZEGI waypoint.

The **Highway Navigation Screen** is designed for those who can go directly to their destination and who want to stay as close to the straight-line course between the two points as possible. Using the highway navigation screen is simple because you just need to follow the road. If you travel directly to the destination, the highway will point straight up. If you stray to the right, the highway points to the left to steer you once more towards the destination. The highway screen was discussed in the Course Deviation Indicator section because it is

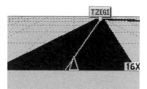

Move to the right to follow the highway and head directly for TZEGI. Turn 23° to the right.

usually combined with CrossTrack Error information. Some receivers allow the user to program the amount of CrossTrack Error allowed before an alarm sounds. Other receivers simply show the highway on the screen and display the CrossTrack Error as a number and a letter "L" or "R". The number is how far you are from the desired course and the letter is whether you are to the left or the right of the desired course.

Map Screens

Built-in and downloadable maps have made the map screen the most useful screen of all. The map screen indicates your position relative to all stored waypoints and all information in the built-in or downloadable map. If you download street maps into your receiver, you will see what road you are on. If you down load a topographical map, you will see your elevation and the topology of the surrounding terrain. Map screens offer a lot of options such as:

Amount of detail Base maps can put a lot of information on the screen even to the point of looking cluttered. You can adjust the amount of information displayed on the screen from a small amount of detail to the maximum detail possible. Setting the amount of detail to the minimum leaves an uncluttered screen, but minor roads and towns may not be displayed. When set to the maximum amount of detail, the receiver tries to display as much information on the screen as possible.

Least amount of detail.

Many receivers also provide a feature called auto mode, which lets the receiver determine when a feature such as a waypoint or a minor road should appear on the screen. The auto mode is governed by the overall amount of detail you specify, whether it be more or less, but it places more detailed information on the screen as you zoom in and removes information from the screen as you zoom out. The auto mode adjusts the amount of information to the amount of area displayed on the screen. If the screen is zoomed out to display a large area, only major features are shown such as freeways or large cities. Zooming in to display a smaller area allows minor features to appear on the screen such as minor roads, towns or railways.

Most amount of detail.

If there is some information that you do not ever need or want to see on the map, turn that information off. For example, you may want to turn off the small cities and towns, so they are not displayed on the screen. Or you could disable local road names, railroads or tide stations if displaying them clutters the screen and they are not important to you.

Selecting north up orientation.

Auto zoom Enabling the auto zoom mode allows the receiver to automatically zoom in if your speed decreases, to provide more details on the map, or to zoom out to show a larger area as your speed increases. The auto zoom mode should be enabled wherever possible.

Orientation The orientation of the map is important during navigation. It can be oriented so that north, your direction of travel, or your destination is always at the top of the screen. North up orientation makes it easier to compare the receiver's map to a paper map or to get oriented in a familiar area. Track up orientation always puts the direction you travel at the top of the screen. As you turn, the map on the screen turns so your direction of travel is always at the top of the screen. If you are in a car on a highway and your destination lies to the right, it is shown to the right on the screen. Track up provides quick reference to where everything is around you, so if a point is on the top of the

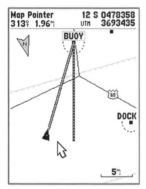

Course up orientation shows the destination "buoy" at the top of the screen. The position marker is to the left of the desired course, so you must turn right to get back to course.

screen it is ahead of you; if at the bottom, it is behind, etc. Course up orientation means that the destination is always at the top of the screen. If you have to get some place and the course is tortuous or if you have complete freedom of movement and can stick to a course, use course up orientation because you can watch your position relative to the destination at the top of the screen. If the symbol representing your position moves to the right of the screen, you are off course to the right and need to move left to get back on course.

Latitude/Longitude grid Turning on latitude/longitude grids displays grid lines on the screen. This function may not be as useful as displaying your current coordinate in the coordinate system of your choice.

Tracks Many receivers regularly store your location in what is known as a track log or track. If the receiver is continuously on during your journey, the track represents your progress along the way. The receiver can be set up to record a waypoint in the track log at a set time interval, a set distance interval or to automatically decide the best method for storing waypoints in the track log, which may be a combination of time or distance depending on your speed and movement. Each entry in the track log contains the waypoint of the location where the entry was recorded and the time it was recorded. It may also contain the elapsed time and distance between track points.

Track log setup menu

Tracks can be transferred from a receiver to a computer. The computer can then display your journey on a map. Track logs can contain hundreds or even thousands of track points. Many receivers allow the track to be reversed and used to navigate back over the path traveled. Tracks are also displayed on the receiver's screen. They can be turned off if they clutter the screen, but they will still be stored as you make your journey.

Tracks are not important if you do not plan on leaving your receiver on during the duration of the trip, but if you do, tracks can accurately show you where you have been and how long it took. Some receivers allow tracks to be saved, much like a route, and used for later navigation. Setting the receiver to store a track and later converting it to a route is a very convenient way to form a route of your trip.

Although many receivers provide a lot of memory for track logs, there is still a finite amount of points that can be stored. If the track log fills up, it can be set to either stop saving new track points or to overwrite the track points stored in memory starting with the points at the beginning of the track. If you want to save a track to later convert into a route, be sure you do not overrun the size of the track log, or you will not have a complete record of your trip.

The track log is very useful in search and rescue operations. Each search team should keep a receiver on and continuously recording the track log. When the team returns, the track can be transferred to a computer as a permanent record of where that team searched.

Scale The scale of the receiver's map can be set from tens of feet to hundreds of miles, which is good because if there is a lot of data in one area from waypoints, the built-in map or a downloaded map, you will need to zoom in to see the details. Many receivers have buttons dedicated to zooming in and out, which makes zooming easy. Zooming is important if the receiver uses downloadable maps, so look carefully at how a receiver zooms before you buy. If zooming is cumbersome or takes a lot of steps, you may want to reconsider buying that model.

Scale = 800 miles.

Customizable Screens

Many receivers allow the user to select the navigational statistics displayed on the screen. Customization of the screens allows you to see what is important to you on a single screen. Your mode of travel determines what information will be important, so customization enables you to use various modes of transportation, whether it be foot or vehicle, and still see all the important information you need without pushing a lot of buttons to page through screens.

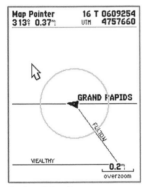

Scale = 0.2 mile.

Flip Screens Receivers with flip screen capabilities allow the user to determine if the display is portrait or landscape. The screens on handheld receivers are usually rectangular. The terms landscape and portrait refer to the screen's orientation when you view it. Most receivers present their information in the portrait format, which means the screen is held so it is taller than it is wide. Landscape means the screen is wider than it is tall. A flip screen allows you to decide how you want to hold, mount and view the receiver. A flip screen is convenient especially when using the map screen because it allows you to decide which aspect displays the information you want to see. If you place the map

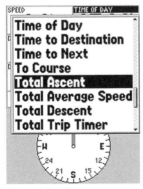

Customizing the screen to show Total Ascent.

screen in the track up mode, the portrait mode allows you to see farther ahead and behind while the landscape mode shows more to each side. Some screens are also easier to see in one mode or the other. A flip screen offers greater viewing options.

Multitone or Color LCD Screens Most receivers now have multitone screens, which means that instead of having only black and white, they have black, white and shades of gray. Some receivers have full color screens, which makes them much easier to read and understand; however, color adds a lot to the price of a receiver. Fortunately, multitone screens provide enough distinction to make reading the screen easy.

Some receivers allow the user to determine if either the land or the water will have a dark shade of gray for its background. If you travel primarily on land, you do not want the land to have a dark background because it obscures the marked waypoints. If you travel primarily on water, you want the water to have a light background because you want to see the details of the water.

Portrait is the most common viewing aspect. A landscape perspective is shown at top.

Water has dark background. Land has light background.

Water has light background. Land has dark background.

Power Sources

Batteries

Although most receivers use only two AA batteries and can last up to 22 hours before needing a change, there are a few things you can do to conserve energy. If you are on foot, use the receiver only when you need a position fix to locate your position either on a paper map or on a downloadable map. Keeping the receiver off most of the time clearly saves on batteries. Another method of saving battery power is to limit its use at night. Most receivers use a type of screen called a liquid crystal display (LCD). If you want to see the screen at night, you have to turn on a small light bulb behind the screen called the "backlight." The backlight quickly drains the batteries, so use it sparingly. If you use your receiver in a vehicle, purchase and use the cigarette-lighter power cord.

Changing the Batteries Do not worry about losing data when you need to change the batteries. Most receivers have a small internal battery that maintains the data even when the AA batteries are removed for an extended period of time. Other receivers use a special type of memory called "flash memory" that never loses its data regardless of how long the batteries have been dead. Unless the receiver specifically states that data will be lost if the batteries go dead, do not worry about it.

External Power If external power is available, like a cigarette lighter in a vehicle, use it. You have to purchase the external power cord, but it allows you to leave the receiver, and even the backlight, on all the time. External power saves you the expense of replacing batteries frequently and allows the receiver to become a true navigational aide that you will really appreciate the more you use it.

Cigarette lighter power adaptor.

Miscellaneous Functions

Initialization

When the receiver is turned on for the first time or after it has been off for several months, it needs to know its approximate location to be able to lock onto the satellites. Most receivers make initialization simple by allowing you to select your approximate position from a list of countries in the world and their corresponding states or cities. Some receivers allow you to select your approximate position from the built-in map. Finally, some receivers ask you to type in your approximate coordinate.

When you first start up a receiver, it may take up to 12.5 minutes before it locks onto the satellites and provides a position. The satellites broadcast the current position of all the satellites. The receiver maintains a record of the satellite positions in its memory. When a receiver first starts up, it listens to the position broadcast to determine if the position information in its memory is current. If it is current, the receiver knows where the satellites are and can immediately start searching for available satellites and calculating its position. If its position data is old, it has to get fresh position data from the satellites before it can do anything. Downloading fresh position data is what takes a long time. The time it takes from the moment you turn the receiver on to the time it calculates its position is called Time To First Fix (TTFF).

Temperature Range

Receivers have maximum and minimum temperature ranges and are not guaranteed to work outside of their stated range. If you work in extreme temperatures, buy a receiver designed for the range it will experience.

The limiting component of a GPS receiver is the liquid crystal display (LCD). Cold temperatures make them fade and work sluggishly and if it is cold enough it will freeze. When using a receiver in cold weather, you may have to keep it warm inside your jacket and take it out when you need a position fix.

Man-Overboard (MOB)

The man-overboard function is useful if you have to quickly mark a spot, so you can return to it later. Imagine you are in your boat, traveling across a lake at night, when suddenly you hear a cry that indicates someone just fell overboard. Being a quick thinker, you press the MOB button. The receiver immediately records your present position, then it instantly switches to the navigation screen to direct you back to the location just recorded. By the time you slow down and get the craft turned around, the receiver is already pointing the direction and distance to return.

When you arrive at the MOB waypoint location, you start the search.

The usefulness of the MOB function is not limited to boats. Imagine you are an archaeologist. You just spotted something resembling an ancient Mayan temple when the base camp calls on the radio. It is a dire emergency and there is no time to lose in getting back to camp. You press the MOB button, jump in the jeep and rush back. Later the receiver will guide you back to the ruin.

Mounting

All manufacturers sell hardware to mount their receivers. It has been mentioned before that most receivers can be set on a car's dash

A mounting bracket holding a receiver.

and pick up the satellite signals through the window. Mounting hardware fixes the receiver to the vehicle, so sudden turns or stops do not send it flying. Mount the receiver within reach of the driver or pilot so they can press the buttons and see the receiver's screen. A receiver mounted deeper inside the vehicle will make it impossible to pick up the satellite signals without an external antenna, so be prepared to purchase both the mounting hardware and the external antenna.

Weight

Advances in electronics have made the weight of GPS receivers a non-issue. Most modern receivers, even the more powerful ones, run on 2 AA or AAA batteries, weigh 3–7 ounces and easily fit in your pocket. Generally, the weigh of a receiver is tied to the size of its screen and the number of batteries it uses. If you are on foot, you will want a smaller, lighter receiver that uses the batteries sparingly. If you are in a vehicle, you will want the largest screen you can get regardless of the weight or power consumption. If you travel in a vehicle most of the time, but occasionally need a receiver in the field, you can find both smaller and larger

Modern receivers are small and lightweight.

models that accept downloadable electronic street maps for use on the road or topographical maps for use in the field. There are some in-between models that weigh 8 to 10 ounces that have larger screens and are reasonable on the batteries. You will be able to find a receiver to meet your use and preference requirements.

Data Entry Keys

The data entry keys on receivers range from buttons on the face to buttons on the sides and even the mouse like button found on portable computers. The characteristic they all have in common is that they are small, so if you have to use a receiver in cold weather with your gloves on, use a pencil or something else to press the buttons because your gloved hand will not be able to do it.

Some receivers can also be set to beep each time a key is pressed. If you use a receiver in the dark, the backlight illuminates the screen, but not the keys. If the receiver beeps with every button press, you can be sure you really hit the key even when it is dark and you cannot see it.

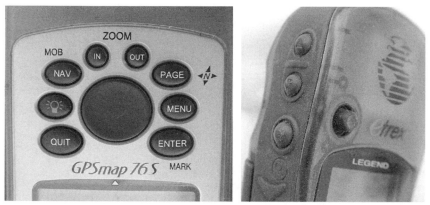

Some receivers have a button similar to a joy stick that facilitates cursor movement on the screen. Others use buttons on the side or on top.

Lanyard Attachment

If you plan to use your receiver while ski touring, or while backpacking with two poles, make sure there is a lanyard attachment point built into the case so you can hang the receiver around your neck while navigating. Some of the receivers are now very small so a lanyard will also help to prevent your losing it.

Calculations

Solar and Lunar Calculations

Many receivers can calculate the times of sunrise, sunset, moonrise, moonset and moon phase based on the date and location. If you are planning an expedition months in advance or to an unfamiliar area, it is nice to know when it will be light or dark or if the moon will provide any light at night.

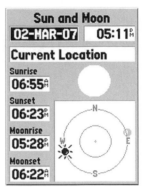

A full moon most of the night contributes to good hunting and fishing.

Hunting and Fishing

Some receivers predict the best times for hunting and fishing for a specific date at a specific location. Unless specifically stated otherwise, the predictions for good hunting and fishing times correspond to the amount of light available for the activity and not to any knowledge of animal behavior. A GPS receiver can accurately calculate the rising and setting of the sun and the moon. It can accurately calculate the moon's phases. It knows nothing about cloud cover, temperature, or ecological conditions. Unless the manufacturer specifically builds additional capability into a receiver, it cannot know about the feeding habits of fish or the migration habits of elk or deer. The receiver's prediction about the best times for hunting and fishing is a statement about the best time for you to be out in the field.

Good hunting and fishing is predicted during the day.

Tides

If you boat or paddle on the ocean, you will want a receiver capable of calculating the tides. Ocean tides are caused primarily by the pull of the moon's gravitational force on the earth. GPS receivers can accurately calculate the moon's movements, so it can also predict the tide.

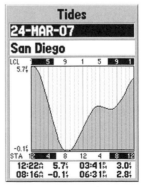

The tide will be out at 8:00 am in San Diego, USA.

Coordinate by Reference or Projection

The coordinates of a waypoint can be calculated by specifying the bearing and distance from any other waypoint. Suppose you are on the safety patrol at a ski resort when a scared, exhausted skier arrives at the lodge. There has been an accident and all the skier can tell you is that he came from "that" direction and skied for about an hour to get to the lodge. You get out your compass to get a bearing of the direction indicated by the person and make a rough estimate of the speed and distance traveled. The lodge's coordinate is already stored in the receiver, so you create a new waypoint for the accident site that is the distance you estimated

Projecting a bearing at 20.34 km (12.6 mi) and 90° from your current location.

at the bearing you measured from the lodge. The receiver calculates the location's waypoint based on that information. Now you can use the calculated coordinate to easily find the location on a map and start a rescue operation close to the probable accident site.

Some receivers with built-in electronic compasses allow the user to face the direction the coordinate should be projected instead of typing in a bearing.

Area Calculations

Some receivers can calculate the area between several waypoints or inside the track lines made during your trip. The points used to define the area must form a closed area for the calculation to be done, which means that a straight line of either waypoints or track points cannot be used to calculate an area.

Time

Each GPS satellite has an ultra-precise atomic clock, so they keep very accurate time. The time maintained by the satellites is called GPS time, and each receiver knows how to convert GPS time to Universal Time Coordinated (UTC), which is the same as Greenwich Mean Time and Zulu time. There is a difference between GPS and UTC time. The GPS clocks started at zero hour on January 6, 1980. Because leap seconds are not used in GPS time, GPS time is now 13 seconds ahead of UTC time. Thirteen seconds does not seem like much, but when making observations, be sure to use UTC and not GPS time. Receivers allow the user to add or subtract an offset to UTC time according to the time zone of your location, which allows the receiver to display the local time. You can also select either a 12-hour or a 24-hour format.

Data Entry

Handheld GPS receivers are designed to be as small as possible, so they do not have a keyboard like a computer. Unless you do all your data entry on a computer then transfer it to the receiver, you have to type in one number or letter at a time. Data entry is straightforward and fairly fast because receivers either serially cycle through the alphabet or provide a table of the alphabet that reduces the number of keystrokes required to type in a name.

Data entry was briefly described under the heading Waypoint Manipulation. An example of entering a new waypoint using both the serial and the tabular method is given here.

Serial Data Entry

You want to mark your present location and give it the name CATLAN. When you press the mark button, some receivers are immediately ready to accept data input while others require that you also press the ENTER button. Once the receiver is ready to accept characters, press the up arrow once and the display will show "A" as the first letter. The display becomes:

A _ _ _ _ _

Each time the up arrow is pressed, the display advances to the next letter in the alphabet. If the down arrow is pressed, the display reverts to the previous letter. Press the up arrow one more time to get the letter "B," then once again to get the letter "C" as the first character. You now see:

C _ _ _ _ _

The first letter is now the one you want, so press the right arrow button to move to the place where the second character will appear.

Use the up and down arrows to select the second letter. Because the second letter is an "A," selecting it requires only one press of the up arrow. Press the right arrow again to move to the location of the third letter.

Tabular Data Entry

Once again, you want to mark a waypoint as CATLAN, but this time your receiver presents the alphabet in table form instead of serially. You press the mark button or select the mark icon from the screen and the receiver presents a screen that includes the place where you need to type in the name and the alphabet in table form. Usually, the letter "A" is highlighted. Use the receiver's buttons to highlight the letter "C" then select it and "C" appears on the screen. Move the cursor back to the letter "A" and select it. Moving from "A" to the letter "L" is where you see the real savings of the table over the serial entry mode. You should be able to get from "A" to "T" in eight or fewer button presses depending on the table layout. Remember that if you move the cursor off the top of the table, it wraps around to the letters at the bottom of the table or if you move off the left of the table, the cursor wraps to the extreme right column in the table. Moving off the edge of the table to get to the other side saves key strokes.

Select all the letters in the waypoint name, and then press the button that tells the receiver to accept it.

Move to the letter "C" and select it.

Move to and select "A".

Press OK to accept waypoint.

5 Using UTM Coordinates on a Hiking Trip

Planning any excursion in the outdoors starts with using a map, whether it is paper or electronic, to decide where you want to go and the route you will take. In unfamiliar country you cannot always tell from the map if the route is feasible, so you consider alternatives. You follow the same process when using a GPS receiver for navigation. You take the coordinates of significant locations from the map and store them in the receiver. When you are out on your trip you combine the information from the GPS receiver with traditional navigational skills to find your way. After introducing you to the UTM grid, this chapter concentrates on how to enter waypoints, how to form a route that your receiver can use and finally, how to use the receiver while hiking.

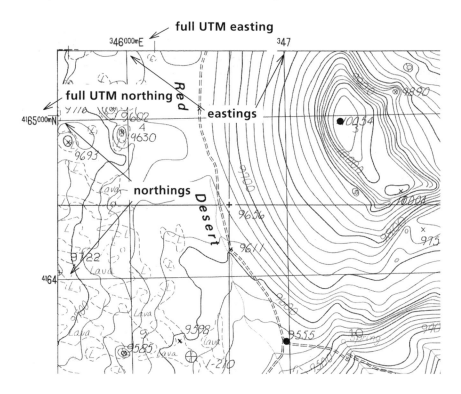

Introduction to the UTM Grid

Enough information on UTM coordinates is given in this chapter for you to determine the coordinate for any point on a map and to use the coordinates with a GPS receiver. Additional information on the UTM grid is given in Chapter 6. The latitude/longitude grid is explained in Chapter 8.

All maps have a grid that uniquely defines every point on the map. The topographical map shown on page 76 is the northwest corner of Henrie Knolls quadrangle, Utah (7.5 minute series, scale 1:24,000). It is printed with the UTM grid and has tick marks for the latitude/longitude and state grids.

The lines that are indicated with arrows form the UTM grid. The numbers along the top of the map are called eastings, which provide an east–west position. The numbers on the left side of the map are called northings. They give you a north–south position. Here is a quick introduction to eastings, northings and UTM coordinates.

Eastings

- Increasing easting numbers means you are going east.
- Full easting coordinate number: 346000m.E.
- Distance between 346000m.E. and 347000m.E. is 1000 m (1 km).
- The large numbers are an abbreviation. On this map:

  46 means 346000m.E.
  47 means 347000m.E.
  Distance between 46 and 47 is 1000 m (1 km).

- The last three numbers stand for meters.
  Distance between 347180m.E. and 347721m.E. is 541 m.
  Distance between 347180m.E. and 352721m.E. is 5.541 km.

Northings

- Increasing northing numbers means you are going north.
- Full northing coordinate number: 4165000m.N.
- Distance between 4164000m.N. and 4165000m.N. is 1000 m (1 km).
- The large numbers are an abbreviation. On this map:

  64 means 4164000m.N.
  65 means 4165000m.N.
  Distance between 64 and 65 is 1000 m (1 km).

- The last three numbers stand for meters.
  Distance between 4164300m.N. and 4164560m.N. is 260 m.
  Distance between 4164300m.N. and 4202560m.N. is 38.260 km.

The UTM grid is based on meters and the grid lines are always 1 km (0.62 mi.) apart on large scale maps. It is easy to estimate distance on a map with the UTM grid because there is a known distance between each grid line. As you will see in Chapter 8, the latitude/longitude grid does not correlate so directly to physical distance.

UTM Coordinates

- The form of a UTM coordinate is zone, easting and northing.
- The zone is printed on the map. For this map it is 12.
- For some receivers, the zone is "12 S" or "12 N." See Chapter 6.
- The complete UTM coordinate of the hill 10,054 ft. is

    12 347400m.E. 4164900m.N., or including the zone letter,
    12 S 347400m.E. 4164900m.N.
    Abbreviated: 47⁴ E. 64⁹ N.

- The complete UTM coordinate of the junction between two unimproved roads with the elevation 9555 ft. is

    12 346900m.E. 4163600m.N., or including the zone letter,
    12 S 346900m.E. 4163600m.N.
    Abbreviated: 46⁹ E. 63⁶ N.

For an explanation of the zone letter "S" see pages 92–94.

Guidebooks that utilize maps with a UTM grid sometimes identify unnamed features by their abbreviated UTM coordinate. Accordingly, the intersection of the roads would be referred to as Grid Reference (GR) 469636 and the hill GR 474649.

Accuracy of UTM Grids

Some recreational users question the accuracy of UTM grids. The UTM grid is a projection of the earth's curved surface onto flat sheets of paper, and as a result there are some inaccuracies across each of the 60 zones (see the explanation of zones in Chapter 6). However, the error is so small that it is of no concern to users of civilian handheld receivers. The inaccuracies of GPS receivers due to ionospheric interference and satellite geometry described on pages 26–27 far outweigh the inaccuracies of the UTM grid.

If you really need to correct for inaccuracies in the grid, some receivers allow you to enter a value for grid declination, which is the difference between grid north and true north. Some maps, including many of the USGS 7.5 minute series, have the angular difference between grid and true north printed on the map (see figure on page 50).

UTM and a GPS Receiver

You now know enough about the UTM grid to read coordinates from a map, however, there are a few points about using UTM coordinates with a receiver.

RIVER waypoint.

- GPS receivers need the complete coordinate numbers. Abbreviations are too map specific. For example, the coordinate for RIVER is entered as

    12 S 0544296E 3629614N

- When entering the coordinates, you do not enter the "m.E." or "m.N." If they are displayed by the receiver as part of the coordinate, they show up automatically without you doing anything.

- Some receivers require seven digits for both easting while others require only six digits for the easting. The first digit in a seven digit easting should always be zero.

REEL waypoint.

- When taking coordinates from a paper map without using a ruler, try to be accurate to within 50 or 100 m. A larger scale maps makes it easier to estimate to 50 m, while smaller scale maps are more easily estimated to 100 m. For example, if the exact coordinate of a landmark is

    12 S 506913m.E. 4615672m.N.

it is visually estimated, depending on the map's scale, and entered into the receiver as

    12 S 506900 4615670 or
    12 S 506900 4615660 or
    12 S 506900 4615680

TZEGI waypoint.

When measuring coordinates off a paper map using a ruler, be as accurate as the ruler allows. Rulers for smaller-scale maps (1:24k, 1:25k) generally have 2 m resolution. Rulers for large-scale maps (1:63.36k, 1:50k) have marks every 50 or 100 metres. Electronic maps provide coordinates in 1 m intervals.

A Hiking Trip in the Mountains

Navigation Plan

The route used in this example could be navigated using compass alone because of the easily visible landmarks such as mountains and streams. However, it illustrates how a GPS receiver complements your present navigation skills and provides increased accuracy. The scenario shows when and why you should rely on the receiver alone, and when it is appropriate to use a compass and altimeter. The example also demonstrates that all aspects of a trip cannot be planned in advance. At one point you have to cross a stream, but you have never been there before and do not know the best place to cross, so your plan allows you to search for a crossing place and still stay on course.

The trip's waypoints are marked on the map on the next page. You will arrive by helicopter at the lake near point #1 in late June. You will arrive late in the afternoon and will want to set up camp before the sun goes down, so you use your receiver to calculate the sunrise and sunset. You discover the sun rises at 4:30 am and sets at 9:28 pm. You arrange the helicopter to drop you off two hours before sunset and plan to get up at sunrise the next morning to catch some fish in the lake. The ultimate destination is point #8, but you plan to take two days to get there because you will photograph wildflowers along the way and want to leave time to search

B-LAKE sunrise/sunset.

for the rare Alpine poppy that grows on Calumet Ridge. The first day's hike will take you from point #1 to #6 where you will camp overnight. The next day you will continue to point #8 where you will join your colleagues for four weeks of botanical studies at a well-established camp. The bush in the area is a dense spruce, so you plan to stay above tree line as much as possible.

Your navigation plan combines your GPS receiver with a compass and altimeter for three reasons. The first is to conserve the receiver's batteries because you will be gone a month and will only have one fresh set for the return trip. The second reason is because part of the trip is through brush and you do not know if the receiver can pick up the satellite signals through the foliage. The third reason is to have a backup navigation method in case a caribou steps on your receiver or something else happens to break it.

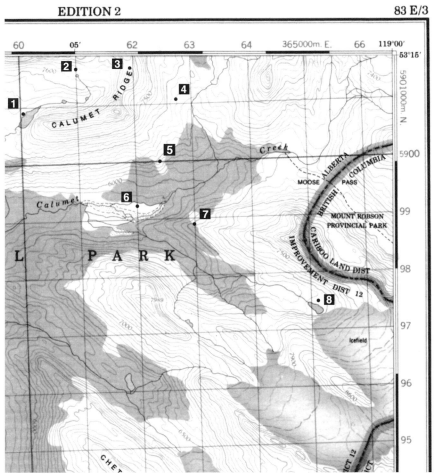

Northeast corner of Mount Robson, British Columbia, Canada (1:50,000 scale).

The terrain determines which tool you will use for navigation once you finally get there, but you have an advance plan all thought out.

- **Travel from point #1 to point #2:**
  Use the GPS receiver the entire way.
  Do not use a compass as you wish to go directly to the lake.
  The receiver will keep you on the right course thereby saving energy and time.

- **Travel from point #2 to point #3:**
  Use the GPS receiver the entire way.
  You want to go directly to the top of the ridge.
  The receiver will keep you on the right course thereby saving energy and time.

- **Travel from point #3 to point #4:**
  Use the compass and altimeter.
  You do not need to get exactly to #4.
  You will be descending steep scree with intermittent cliff bands. In mist this will be tricky and time consuming. Use the compass to walk toward #4 until you reach an altitude of 6,800 ft.

- **Travel from point #4 to point #5:**
  Use the altimeter with the GPS receiver occasionally.
  You want to travel almost in a straight line from #4 to #6.
  Point #5 is situated just before you enter the trees. You want to arrive as close to #5 as possible.
  Use the altimeter to drop gradually to an altitude of 6,400 ft. until you approach the trees.
  Once you are close to the trees, check your position with the receiver. If necessary, use the receiver's Goto function to guide you the last part of the leg to #5.

- **Travel from point #5 to point #6:**
  Use the compass.
  You have to walk through trees and you do not know if your receiver will work, so you plan to rely on your compass.
  Walk the bearing between #5 and #6.
  When you reach the clearing at the creek, use the receiver to verify your position.

- **Travel from point #6 to point #7:**
  Use the compass and altimeter.
  You are not sure where you can cross Calumet Creek as the runoff is high. Follow it upstream until it can be crossed.
  Cross the creek and try to get a new location reading using the receiver.
  If it can lock onto the satellites, get a position fix and walk the bearing from your present position to the tree line at #7.
  If the trees block the satellite signals, travel southeast, true north reference not magnetic, to the tree line.

- **Travel from point #7 to point #8:**
  Use the compass and receiver.
  Contour along at tree line and the stream when you arrive at it, until you reach the upper valley where the terrain levels off.
  Use the receiver to get an occasional fix, but for the most part, follow the stream to the lake.
  In good weather the entire route could be navigated by sight.
  However, in thick cloud or driving rain the receiver is very useful.

Entering Waypoints

The plan looks feasible, so it is time to enter all the waypoints into the receiver. Even though the receiver is not used to guide you to every waypoint, there are several good reasons to enter them into the receiver's memory. The first is because the receiver automatically calculates the bearing between each point. Of course, you could measure the bearings from the map, but it is so much easier with the receiver, especially when it automatically compensates for declination. The receiver can also calculate the distance between each waypoint. Only the route between #7 and #8 is not direct, so the sum of the distances between each point, as calculated by the receiver, will be close to the actual distance traveled. Because the receiver does not include changes of altitude in its distance calculation, it is impossible to get a complete picture of the hike's difficulty, but the total distance does provide an indication. Most receivers show your present position and any waypoints stored in memory on the map screen. A final reason to store the coordinates of each point in the memory is to prepare for the possibility of bad weather, which would mandate more reliance on the receiver than anticipated.

Use the map to estimate the UTM coordinates for each point to the closest 50 to 100 m. One hundred meters is one tenth of the UTM square grid shown on the map. The waypoints are represented by the dot next to the numbers on the map. The UTM coordinate for each point, rounded to the nearest 100 m, is given below along with a name:

Point	Zone	Easting	Northing	Name
#1	11 U	360100m.E.	5900800m.N.	B-LAKE
#2	11 U	361000m.E.	5901600m.N.	S-LAKE
#3	11 U	361900m.E.	5901800m.N.	CRIDGE
#4	11 U	362700m.E.	5901100m.N.	FLAT
#5	11 U	362400m.E.	5900000m.N.	WOODS
#6	11 U	362000m.E.	5899300m.N.	STREAM
#7	11 U	363000m.E.	5898800m.N.	ORIDGE
#8	11 U	365200m.E.	5897500m.N.	CAMP

Before you enter the data, initialize the receiver to the following settings:

- **Map datum: North American Datum 1927 (NAD 27)**
  If your receiver splits NAD 27 into separate settings for Alaska, Canada, Central America, etc., select NAD 27-Canada, otherwise, select NAD 27.

- **Units: Metric**
  The UTM grid is based on the meter, so it is much easier to use the map if the distance is also set to metric units.

- **Coordinate grid: UTM**
- **North setting: Magnetic North**
  A compass is used to get between several points. If the receiver is set to report direction as magnetic bearings, they can be directly dialed into the compass without compensating for the declination.
- **CDI limit: Small**
  If the Course Deviation Indicator's tolerance is selectable, set it somewhere between 250 to 500 m. The receiver's Goto function will be used to navigate to points #2 and #3. A CDI limit of 250 to 500 m means you will stray at most 250 or 500 m from course before the receiver will warn you.
- **WAAS setting: Off**
  As you are in an area where there is no WAAS coverage, turn WAAS off so as to not introduce error.

At last, the coordinates of each point can be entered into the receiver. The points entered on this trip will be formed into a route, not because the route function will be used, but because the receiver automatically calculates the distance and bearing between each point in a route and you want to know the bearing to use with your compass. Each receiver displays routes differently, but the information that all of them provide is shown below. The desired track is the bearing of the straight line between the two points. The distance is expressed in kilometers because the receiver's units were set to metric.

Name	Point	Desired Track	Distance km
B-LAKE	#1		
		27°	1.2
S-LAKE	#2		
		56°	0.9
CRIDGE	#3		
		110°	1.1
FLAT	#4		
		174°	1.1
WOODS	#5		
		188°	0.8
STREAM	#6		
		95°	1.1
ORIDGE	#7		
		99°	2.6
CAMP	#8		

Each segment in a route is called a leg. The distance of the first five legs of the trip, from B-LAKE to STREAM, is 5.1 km (3.2 mi.), while the total distance, if hiked in a straight line between each point, is 8.8 km (5.5 mi.). The receiver is now ready for the trip and you are ready to test it in the field.

In the Field

The day finally arrives. After a spectacular flight, the helicopter lands near the lake and you disembark with plenty of time to set up camp. Just as planned, you are fishing the lake the next morning at 4:00 and catch a fine breakfast. When it is time to go, you turn the receiver on, but it seems to take much longer than usual to lock onto the satellites. When a receiver loses its memory, has not been used for a few months or when it is moved more than 300 miles from the location where it last locked, it can take up to 12.5 minutes for a receiver to get a position fix. The time between turning the receiver on and locking on to the satellites is known as Time To First Fix (TTFF) and was described in Chapter 4. The next thing you notice is that the altitude is not even close to the value stated on the map. You knew that the accuracy of the altitude would not be good enough for reliable navigation, so you brought along an electronic altimeter that looks like a watch. From the map, you determine your altitude is about 7,200 ft. and you calibrate your altimeter by setting its altitude to 7,200 ft. Manufacturers of electronic altimeters are listed in the back of the book in the Resources section.

It is time to get going, so you activate the Goto function and tell the receiver to guide you to point #2, which is named S-LAKE. As you walk along, the receiver reports that the desired track, as you already knew from the route information above, is 27° and your track is also 27°. The compass navigation screen has the arrow pointing straight ahead, which means you are right on track.

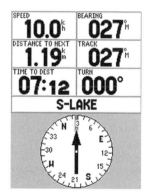

Compass screen to S-LAKE.

85

After a while, you start to look around for wildflowers and do not pay much attention to the receiver. Once you finally look at it, you notice your direction is now 38° and the arrow on the compass screen points to the left, which means you need to turn to the left to head directly to S-LAKE. You also notice that the bearing to get to the lake has changed from 27° to 24°.

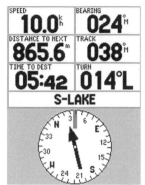

Before you correct your course, you switch to the highway screen and continue walking just to see what happens. After a short distance, the highway screen shows you are off the straight line course by 62.0 m. The triangle shape represents your position. It lies to the right of the line going up the highway a distance of 62.0 m. The darker area represents the path leading to S-LAKE. The lighter line in the middle of the path represents the straight line from where you pressed the Goto button to S-LAKE. You also notice you have wandered so far afield that the bearing to S-LAKE is now 22° and not 24°. The TURN statistic informs you that you must turn 16° to the left to travel directly to S-LAKE.

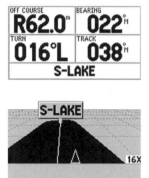

Then you switch to the map screen. It shows both B-LAKE and S-LAKE with a straight line representing the desired, direct course between them. Your position is marked by the triangle. The line from the triangle to S-LAKE is the direct course from your current position to the destination. Being off course slightly is not really a problem. You simply turn your direction of travel to the left to a bearing of 20° and keep going. The triangle turns to show that you are headed directly towards S-LAKE. You note that your estimated time en route (ETE) is about 5 minutes, so it will not be long before you arrive.

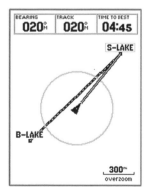

But then you start to wander again. There are more flowers with greater variety than you expected. With a few stops here and a quick picture over there, you soon find you are walking a bearing of 352° and the arrow on the compass screen points to the right, which means you need to follow the arrow to the right to travel toward S-LAKE. So much for going directly to the lake as you had planned. There is just too much to see and do.

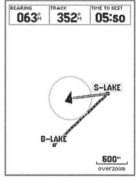

You switch to the map screen. Your wanderings took you off course to the left. The bearing to S-LAKE is now 63°. You will have to turn to the right to get to S-LAKE, but you just spotted a large patch of wildflowers farther to the left and you must go see them. You watch the screen as you walk to the flowers. You are getting farther and farther off course to the left of the original straight line between B-LAKE and S-LAKE. By the time you reach the flowers, you are 427 m from course, but the flowers are beautiful and after you take pictures, you switch to the highway screen, determined to go straight from where you are now to S-LAKE.

You turn to the right until the TURN statistic shows 0°. Walking a track of 74° shows the S-LAKE waypoint straight ahead on the highway screen. You can still see the dark road with its white center line because you are not so far off course that it is off the screen.

You stay on the bearing leading to S-LAKE and soon the receiver beeps and announces that you are getting close to the destination. You can see the lake to the right and it is approximately 100 m away, just like you planned when you picked the coordinate for the S-LAKE waypoint. You continue on the course until the screen shows your position directly at S-LAKE.

You plan to use the Goto function to get from S-LAKE to CRIDGE, so you activate Goto and select CRIDGE as the destination. The compass screen shows that you must bear to the right to go straight to CRIDGE.

You switch to the map screen where you can see the B-LAKE, CRIDGE, FLAT, WOODS, STREAM and ORIDGE waypoints along with your current position at S-LAKE as a triangle. Out of curiosity, you move the map cursor, the white arrow, so it touches the ORIDGE waypoint. The map screen adds a new line of information that tells you that you are 3.44 km from ORIDGE at a bearing of 123°. It also gives the UTM coordinate of where the cursor is pointing, which in this case is the ORIDGE waypoint. You move the cursor to several other locations on the map and see the distance, bearing and coordinate. If a downloadable electronic map had been available for the area, it would have been easy to plan the trip and get the waypoint coordinates using the receiver instead of using a paper map, but unfortunately, electronic maps are not available for some of the more beautiful places.

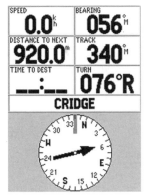

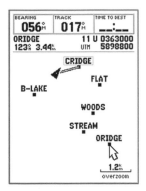

You now have a much better understanding of how to do basic navigation using your GPS receiver. You start by measuring the coordinate of the location you want to visit from a map, entering it into the receiver's memory and activating the Goto navigation function. The receiver guides you to the point along a straight line from your present position to the destination. If you do not travel directly to the destination, the receiver tells you not only how far you are off course, but what correction to make to head directly to the destination again.

You were walking a bearing of 75° when you arrived at S-LAKE, but the bearing to CRIDGE from S-LAKE is 56°, so the highway in the navigation screen points to the right showing that you need to change your course and hike off to the right.

On this leg, you pay a lot more attention to the receiver and you are able to hold the bearing exactly. You are progressing fine until you get about halfway to CRIDGE, when you encounter a very boggy section of ground. Your foot sinks so deep into the mud that you doubt you will be able to make it across without getting stuck, or worse, without falling down. You scan the horizon and notice solid ground far to the left that may provide passage.

You decide to leave your receiver on just to see what the navigation screen says as you take the long detour to get around the mud. To get to the solid ground, you travel at an angle of 90° off the straight line between S-LAKE and CRIDGE, which makes your bearing 326°. The arrow in the compass navigation screen signals a hard right, but there is nothing you can do to follow the course indicated by the receiver as long as you are walking around the mud. You switch to the highway screen to discover that you are so far off course that the middle of the highway does not even appear on the screen; however, the TURN statistic shows that you just turn 90° to the right to return to course and the bearing from your current position to CRIDGE is still 56°.

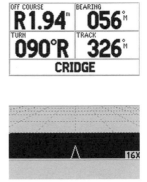

At long last you reach the rock and you switch to the map screen to see that you really went a long way off course to get past the mud, but the beauty of the GPS receiver is that you know exactly where you are and the bearing to CRIDGE is now 97°. Taking the detour with

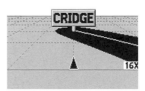

compass alone and still getting to CRIDGE would be much more difficult. The rest of the way is fairly flat and it all looks like solid rock, so you should be able to go from where you are directly to the destination. You look at the highway navigation screen. You are off course to the left by 431 m. You can see the highway with its white center line and you can also see that you now are headed directly for CRIDGE.

The compass and highway steering screens each play their part. The highway screen shows how close you are to the straight line between two points and the compass screen always tells you which direction to go regardless of your proximity to the direct course. The highway screen is best used in conditions where you have the freedom of movement to always maintain the direct course to the destination, like on water or in the air. The compass screen works well in situations where you have to go around obstacles that lie in the straight line path. Paying attention, you continue from your present position and quickly arrive at point CRIDGE. A look at the map screen also shows the detour you had to make.

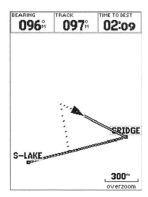

The plan to get to FLAT is to walk in the general direction until you reach an altitude of 6,800 ft. The bearing between CRIDGE and FLAT is 110° with reference to the magnetic pole, so you turn the compass housing until the number 110 lines up with the direction arrow, you take a sighting and start to walk. Your altimeter reads 8,180 ft., which corresponds closely to the map. Point CRIDGE does not lie directly on any of the map's altitude lines, but you know it is somewhere between 8,100 ft. and 8,200 ft. The altimeter updates its electronic readout only once every two minutes, but the descent is not steep and the readout is generally up-to-date. When the altimeter reads 6,900 ft., you take a two minute break and when it updates you discover your altitude is 6,860 ft. The receiver tells you that you are within 100 m of FLAT. With your compass, you sight a bearing of 174° and hike keeping an eye on the altimeter. At 6,400 ft. you are close to the trees and the map screen shows your position very close to the waypoint WOODS, point #5 on the map. Next you sight a bearing of 188° and dive into the bush on the way to STREAM. The plant life is a lot thicker than you thought it would be and after a while you begin to wonder if it would have been faster to have gone around the trees and followed the stream up to the STREAM waypoint. You get out the receiver, but it will not lock because the foliage is so dense. There are no clearings where you might get a GPS fix, so you continue as close as possible on the bearing. Soon you are out of the trees, your receiver locks and the Goto function leads you to the STREAM waypoint, #6 on the map, where you spend the night.

The map screen on the receiver shows your position as a triangle and the locations of the other waypoints. You use the buttons on the receiver to move the map cursor, the white arrow, to the ORIDGE waypoint. The bearing, 95°, and distance, 1.12 km, from your current position to ORIDGE are displayed on the screen along with the coordinate for ORIDGE. The small marks between B-LAKE and CRIDGE represent the data stored in the track log as you used the receiver to navigate between those waypoints. They show that your course between the waypoints was not direct.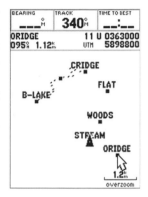

In the morning you execute your plan by following the stream until you find a good place to cross. Once again the receiver will not lock in the bush, so you follow the contingency plan of walking southeast to get out of the trees, but you need to set your compass to get a sighting. You know the declination is east 22° and southeast in relation to true north is 135°. You repeat the phrase "East is least, West is best" to remind yourself that to convert from true north bearings to magnetic, you subtract east declinations and add west declinations. The declination is east, so you subtract 22° from 135° to get the southeast magnetic bearing for the area of 113°. You set your compass and you do your best to get through the bush as fast as possible. Once you are through, you follow the tree line then the stream directly to the lake without using either the compass, altimeter or the receiver. During the next month at the camp, you use the receiver to record the locations of wildflowers and to explore the icefields to the south and east.

When it is time to meet the helicopter, you use the map to plan a new route back to the lake that avoids traveling through the bush.

6 More UTM and Collecting Water Samples in the Desert

The beauty of the Universal Transverse Mercator (UTM) grid is its ease of use. It is simple to read eastings and northings directly from the map in the field without the aid of a ruler. However, there are elements of the UTM grid that need more explanation, such as the origin of the zone number and letter used in the previous chapter.

The UTM grid splits the world into 60 zones that are each 6° wide. Zone 1 starts at west longitude 180°, which is the same as east longitude 180°, as shown in the figure at the top of page 93.

The zone number increases by 1 for every 6° interval until the entire circumference of the world is covered and the last zone, number 60, is reached. As each zone is peeled off the globe and flattened, it loses its relationship to a sphere, so the UTM coordinates are called false coordinates, unlike the latitude/longitude grid, which is a geographic coordinate. The narrow width of the 6° zones reduces distortion when the strips are flattened. The Transverse Mercator projection provides a uniform grid for the entire earth. UTM maps do not cover the areas

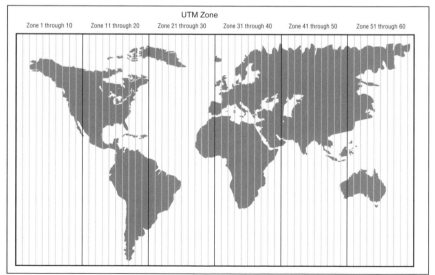

The 60 UTM zones.

around the north pole, above north latitude 84°, and the south pole, below south latitude 80°, because maps of the poles are drawn with the Universal Polar Stereographic (UPS) grid. The UPS grid is discussed in Chapter 15.

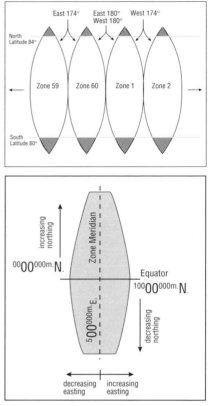

Each UTM zone has horizontal and vertical reference lines. UTM easting coordinates are measured from the line running down the middle of the zone called the zone meridian. Each 6° zone is split directly in two by the zone meridian. Zone 1, as shown in the figure on the right, is bounded by west longitude 180° on the left and west longitude 174° on the right. The middle of the zone lies on the W 177° longitude line, which is 3° toward the center from each side. Zone 2 is bounded by W 174° and W 168° with its zone meridian located at W 171° and so forth for each zone.

UTM zone meridians.

The meridian of every zone is always labeled 500000m.E. An easting greater than 500000m.E. lies east of the meridian, while anything less than that lies to the west. The value of an easting coordinate reveals its distance from the zone meridian in meters. The easting 501560m.E. is 1560 m east of the meridian because it is 1560 greater than 500000m.E.; whereas the easting 485500m.E. is 500,000 - 485,500 = 14,500 m west of the meridian. A valid easting for a given zone will not be less than 166640m.E. or greater than 833360m.E. Easting coordinates always increase as you move east and decrease as you go west.

Northing coordinates are always measured relative to the equator, which is the horizontal reference line in each zone. The northing value assigned to the equator is 0000000m.N. for locations north of the equator and 10000000m.N. for places south of the equator. You have to know if the northing coordinate lies above or below the equator. The methods for describing if a location is above or below the equator are described below. A northing coordinate for a place north of the equator is simply its distance above the equator. A northing value of 5897000m.N. means the point lies

93

5,897,000 m north of the equator. A valid northing for a position above the equator will lie between 00**00**000m.N. and 93**34**080m.N.

The northing coordinates for locations south of the equator also define the position's distance from the equator, but the equator is assigned the northing value of 10**00**000m.N. The northing value 58**97**000m.N. lies 10,000,000 - 5,897,000 = 4,103,000 m south of the equator. Valid northing coordinates for the southern hemisphere lie between 11**10**400m.N., at the very southern end of a zone and 10**00**000m.N. at the equator. Regardless of whether you are above or below the equator, northing values increase as you go north and decrease as you travel south.

GPS receivers use three different ways to express the hemisphere of a UTM coordinate. The coordinates below all describe the exact same place in zone 11.

    11   3**60**100m.E. 59**00**800m.N.
    11 N 3**60**100m.E. 59**00**800m.N.
    11 U 3**60**100m.E. 59**00**800m.N.

The first coordinate does not visually tell the user the hemisphere. When the coordinate was entered into the receiver, it asked for the hemisphere and recorded it in its memory, but it does not display it on the screen. The "N" in the second coordinate indicates that it lies in the northern hemisphere, whereas an "S" appears in the same place if the location is below the equator. In the third coordinate, the letter "U" is from the Military Grid Reference System (MGRS) and specifies position relative to the equator.

The MGRS divides each UTM zone horizontally into 8° sections and assigns letters as shown in the figure opposite. The letter "U" means your position lies somewhere between north latitude 48° and 56°. The word north starts with "N," which will remind you that in the MGRS system the letter "N" and every letter after it specifies a location above the equator. Do not mistake the letter "S" for the southern hemisphere if your receiver uses the MGRS letters.

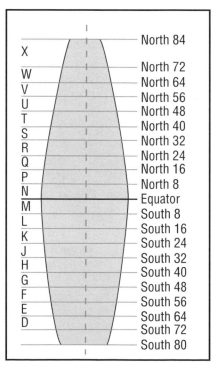

MGRS letters applied to a zone.

UTM Rulers

The point has been made several times that UTM coordinates on a large scale map can easily be read by the unaided eye. However, there are several rulers that make an already easy-to-use grid even simpler. The source of map rulers is found in the back of the book in the Resources section. The UTM Reader and The Card are specifically for the UTM grid.

A typical 1:24,000 UTM grid ruler.

The corner of the ruler is placed at the location where you want to measure the coordinate. The lines of the UTM grid intersect both the vertical and the horizontal scales on the ruler. The figure shows how to measure the UTM coordinate of a building on the USGS Long Branch, NJ topographical map. Note that the horizontal scale is intersected by an easting grid line. The easting coordinate is found by adding the number where the grid crosses the scale to the base number of the easting grid line. In this case the scale is intersected at 480, so the easting coordinate becomes:

$$575000m.E. + 480 = 575480m.E.$$

A northing grid line intersects the vertical scale and the northing coordinate is found in the same way as the easting coordinate was found above. In this example, the vertical scale is crossed at 650 by the $4458000m.N.$ grid line. The northing coordinate becomes:

$$4458000m.N. + 650 = 4458650m.N.$$

The final complete coordinate is

$$18\ T\ 575480m.E.\ 4458650m.N.$$

The coordinates of any location are measured in the same way.

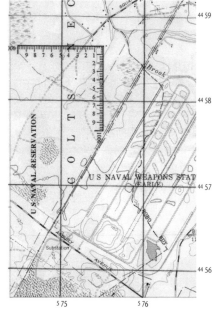

Long Branch, NJ USGS Topo.

Collecting Water Samples in the Desert

Now it is time to take another trip using the UTM grid. This time you need to collect water samples from springs in the Arizona Superstition Wilderness, which is an arid desert. There are distinctive landforms that could help in navigation, but much of the terrain looks similar making it easy to get lost. The GPS receiver will not only keep you from getting lost, it will help you travel the most efficient route.

Motorized vehicles are not usually allowed in the wilderness area, but you have been granted permission to use your four-wheel ATV, which is similar to a motorcycle, because the task needs to be finished fast. The receiver is mounted on the handlebars and is powered by the vehicle's battery, so it will be left on the entire time. The coordinates of all the places you need to go will be entered into the receiver's memory and linked together in a route. When you begin, you will activate the route and the navigation screen will steer you from one site to the next without you even touching the buttons, so you will be able to drive and navigate at the same time. You decide the compass navigation screen is the best for the job because you have to go around obstacles and cannot proceed directly from one point to the next. What you really need to know is the direction from your present position to the destination and the compass screen conveniently provides that information.

Once again, the trip starts with a map. The USGS topographical map of Pinyon Mountain, Arizona (scale 1:24,000) covers the area. Your map is old and does not have the UTM grid printed on it, so you draw the grid lines as indicated by the blue tick marks along the edges. Use a long ruler to line up the tick marks with the same numbers on opposite sides of the map and draw the line all the way across. As in the example of the previous chapter, the grid forms 1 km (0.62 mi.) squares. The zone number, 12, is printed on the map. However, if your receiver requires the MGRS letter to designate the hemisphere and you do not know what it is, you can either find the correct letter from the figure on page 94 or just use the letter "N" to tell the receiver the location is north of the equator. Once you enter the rest of the coordinate, the receiver automatically changes the letter from "N" to "S," which is correct for a receiver that uses the MGRS letter system.

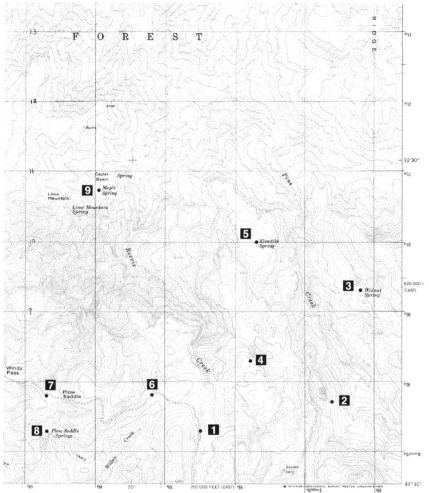

USGS Pinyon Mountains, Arizona. (1:24,000 scale)

Point	Zone	Easting	Northing	Name
#0	12 S	485410m.E.	3704000m.N.	W-00 off map
#1	12 S	485510m.E.	3707300m.N.	W-01
#2	12 S	487390m.E.	3707710m.N.	W-02
#3	12 S	487800m.E.	3709300m.N.	W-03
#4	12 S	486210m.E.	3708300m.N.	W-04
#5	12 S	486300m.E.	3710000m.N.	W-05
#6	12 S	484810m.E.	3707800m.N.	W-06
#7	12 S	483300m.E.	3707800m.N.	W-07
#8	12 S	483300m.E.	3707290m.N.	W-08
#9	12 S	484050m.E.	3710740m.N.	W-09

As always, you must set the receiver properly before entering the waypoints.

- **Map datum: North American Datum 1927 (NAD 27)**
  If your receiver splits NAD 27 into separate settings for Alaska, Canada, Central America, etc., select NAD 27-CONUS (Continental US), otherwise, select NAD 27.

- **Units: Metric**
  The UTM grid is based on the meter and it is much easier to relate distances to the map if the receiver reports them in meters, so set the receiver's units to metric.

- **Coordinate grid: UTM**

- **North setting: True North**
  A compass will not be used to navigate, so set the north reference to true north so the bearings relate to the map.

- **CDI limit: Large**
  The receiver will guide you to all points, but you decided it does not matter how far you are off the straight line course just as long as you know the direction from your present position to the next point. Set the CDI limit to 5 km, so that just in case you decide to look at the highway steering screen, it will still look like a road even if you are a long way off course.

- **WAAS setting: On**
  As you are in an area where there is WAAS coverage, turn WAAS on for increased accuracy.

Using the map, you choose waypoints leading to the springs over terrain that looks passable with the ATV. On your ruler, you find the 1:24K UTM scale and measure the coordinates. The ruler makes it easy to get the coordinates to an accuracy of about 10 m (32.8 ft.). The coordinates for the numbers shown on the map along with their waypoint name are listed on page 97. Waypoint #0 lies on the road south of #1 just off the map. There are additional springs in the area that need testing, but the waypoints listed are enough for a morning's work.

The route for this trip is different from the previous chapter because some waypoints are used more than once. For example, the planned route takes you from #2 to #3 then back to #2 before continuing to #4. Each type of receiver displays routes differently, but the information they all provide is shown below. The desired track is the bearing between two adjacent points. When reading the bearing, remember the north reference was set to true north.

Name	Point	Desired Track	Distance km
W-00	#0		
		2°	3.3
W-01	#1		
		78°	1.9
W-02	#2		
		14°	1.6
W-03	#3		
		194°	1.6
W-02	#2		
		297°	1.3
W-04	#4		
		3°	1.7
W-05	#5		
		288°	2.4
W-09	#9		
		108°	2.4
W-05	#5		
		183°	1.7
W-04	#4		
		250°	1.5
W-06	#6		
		270°	1.5
W-07	#7		
		180°	0.5
W-08	#8		
		0°	0.5
W-07	#7		

The total trip as planned from W-00 to W-07, including all the back-and-forth between the waypoints, is 21.9 km (13.6 mi.). The altitude does not change much over the route, so the distance calculated by the receiver will be close to the actual distance traveled if the terrain allows you to travel directly between the waypoints.

The navigation plan is to use the receiver the entire trip because it will help you finish much faster than if you navigated with compass alone. You will travel on the road shown on the map wherever possible. When traveling from W-00 to W-01 and from W-06 to W-07, stay on the road regardless of where the navigation screen points. When you arrive at W-01, turn off the road and follow the direction indicated by the receiver as closely as possible and do the same when you arrive at W-07. You will carry the map and compass for backup navigation just in case something happens to the receiver.

The week before the trip, you get a bonus at work. Strange as it seems, the amount of the check is for exactly the same amount that it costs to buy the downloadable, electronic topographic maps from the receiver manufacturer. It must be a sign, and even if it is not, you have always wanted downloaded topographic maps, so you rush to the store and buy them. As soon as you get home, you transfer the topographic maps for the area you will travel into your receiver. The day of the trip arrives and after a good night's rest at W-00, you start the ATV and turn the receiver on. The sun is just rising over the horizon making the saguaro cacti cast long shadows. It is going to be a scorcher of a day because there are no clouds in the sky. You find the route where you stored the waypoints and activate it. As you start up the road, the arrow on the compass navigation screen points straight up, which means you are right on course, but soon the road curves to the left. Your direction changes to 342° and the arrow turns slightly to the right showing that you need to turn to the right to go directly to W-01.

You ignore the arrow because you know you need to stay on the road until you reach W-01. The road curves to the right and the compass arrow swings left showing you how to return to the desired course, but you ignore it and press on. Within 0.25 km (0.16 mi.) of W-01, a message flashes on the screen that you are approaching the waypoint, so you slow down and get ready to follow the steering arrow. As soon as you arrive at W-01, the arrow on the navigation screen swings hard to the right and the bearing you are supposed to follow changes to 78°. You turn to the right and begin to go off the road toward W-02. You are able to maintain almost a direct course until you are about half-way there when you notice the terrain to the right is much flatter than the route you planned. You stop to consult the map and decide to veer to the right until the bearing to get to W-02 is 0°, which will put you due south of the waypoint. Then you will turn directly north to get to W-02 before heading off to

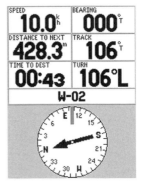

W-03. You follow the easiest path possible and note your new track is about 106°. You had thought about moving W-02 farther south when you were planning the route, but you decided to put it where it is because you thought you could make it up the incline. Now that you are in the field, you see that the southerly route is better. You keep an eye on the bearing to W-02 and when it reaches 0° you make a hard left turn until the arrow in the compass points directly up showing you are headed directly to W-02.

You cannot resist looking at the map screen, so you stop to see the map drawn by the receiver. This shows your present position, a triangular shape, directly south of W-02. It is exactly what you wanted. You move the map cursor, the light-colored arrow, to the contour line directly east of W-02. Its elevation is 4856 ft. It lies at a bearing of 11° and is 624.8 m from your position. Its coordinate is also given as 12 S 487508 3707710. Not only is the downloadable topographical map nice, the map cursor allows you to select and identify the geographical and topographical map information.

Once you arrive at W-02, the receiver automatically starts steering toward W-03, so the bearing you are supposed to follow changes to 14° and the arrow points to the right. As you adjust your course by turning to the right, the arrow in the compass moves until it points straight up and your track is 14°. A third of the way to W-03, you see that the terrain to the east is more easily passable, so you do the exact same thing as before: you will veer to the right until the bearing to get to W-03 is 0°, then you will turn directly north to get to the waypoint. You turn to the right and watch the screen occasionally until the bearing to W-03 is 0°, then you drive due north. A quick look at the receiver's map shows your deviation from course to be small and W-03 lies directly ahead. Within minutes you arrive at Walnut Spring and take the necessary samples.

The receiver is already pointing the way back to W-02 at 194°, but you head due south on a bearing of 180° until the terrain looks passable, then you turn to follow the arrow to W-02. Until you turn to travel directly toward W-02, the arrow increasingly points more to the right. When you arrive at W-02, the receiver directs you to take a right turn to go toward W-04, but you know by looking at the terrain and also from the trip up that you should go due south of W-02 to where the terrain is more level, then turn toward W-04. For now you ignore the arrow and watch your track to make sure it is 180°.

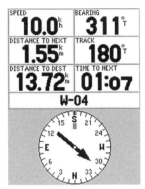

The receiver shows the distance to W-04 increasing, but as soon as you are off the small hill and can finally turn directly toward W-04, the bearing is 311° and you are 1.55 km (0.96 mi.) away. When you arrive at W-04, the receiver points the way to W-05. You adjust your course to 3° and notice that it is going to be a straight shot to Klondike Spring at W-05 because the terrain is fairly level.

After collecting water at the spring, you notice the terrain to W-09 is far rougher than you thought it would be from the map. You take another look at the map and decide to head due west to just past Reevis Creek, then turn almost due north to get to W-09. You will not be watching the compass arrow very closely until the bearing to W-09 is about 316°, but the receiver's map has been very useful during these maneuvers, so you decide to follow the terrain of least resistance and track your progress on the map screen. You travel for a while, then you look at the map. This shows you were headed west, then almost southwest. You are making progress because you are closer to W-09. The terrain is still passable, so you keep going.

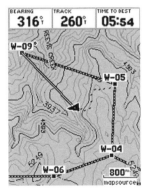

When the bearing to W-09 is about 316°, you turn and head directly for the waypoint. Once you arrive at the waypoint, you look at the map to see the loop you had to make to get there.

After you get the water sample from Maple Spring, the receiver is already pointed back to waypoint W-05. You want to take the same loop to return, so you follow the track marks on the receiver's map. On the trip to W-09, the receiver's map was set to keep north at the top of the screen, but for the trip back you set it to display your direction of travel at the top. This "track up" mode allows you to easily see where you need to turn to stay on the track already drawn on the map.

The path from W-05 back to W-04 is a straight shot over easy terrain, so you switch back to the compass navigation screen and soon find yourself at W-04. The receiver now points directly to W-06. After surveying the terrain, you look again at the map to see that you have to cross Reevis Creek to get to W-06. The planned route might be a bit steep compared to the terrain farther south, but you decide to follow the receiver until you get to the creek and if you cannot cross there, you will travel parallel to the creek until the ground levels enough to cross, then you will follow the receiver's directions straight to W-06. When you get to the creek, you find the sides are really steep, so you drive alongside it in a southward direction until it becomes relatively flat and easy to cross. You look at the receiver's map and see you are almost headed straight for W-01. You could continue to W-01 using the receiver's map screen for guidance then take the road to W-06, but you decide to cross the wash and go directly to W-06. The arrow on the compass navigation screen shows the direct route, so you change your course to 272° and drive straight there. The plan is to take the road from W-06 to W-07, so once on the road, you stay on it regardless of where the compass arrow points until you arrive at W-07. From W-07 you follow the receiver's steering arrow directly to W-08 and take a sample from Plow Saddle Springs. The receiver then directs you back to W-07. The route is now complete, so you deactivate it. You do not really need the receiver anymore because all you need to do is to follow the road back to your camp, but just so you know how long it will take to arrive, you activate the Goto function, select W-00 and watch the estimated time en route (ETE) as you zoom back to your tent.

7 GPS Navigation in a Whiteout

In the previous two chapters, you learned how to use a GPS receiver along with a map to plan your route. Another practical use of GPS technology is as a backup means of navigation in poor weather. You plan to take some friends to the top of Mount Columbia, located in the Canadian Rockies. To get to the peak, you need to cross the Columbia Icefields, which lie at an altitude of 3,038 to 3,353 m (10,000 to 11,000 ft.) and like any high mountain area, they are subject to whiteout conditions that make navigation extremely difficult. Clouds do not affect the satellite signals, so it is a perfect application for a GPS receiver.

Most people who climb Mount Columbia set up a base camp on the northeast side of the icefield. If the weather is bad when they arrive, they stay in camp and wait it out, but if it is clear they carry only their survival gear and hurry across the icefield to the peak. Even though it is clear on the trip to the mountain, it is not unusual for clouds to come up out of the valleys very quickly, resulting in whiteout conditions for the return trip. Preparations for finding your way back in conditions of poor visibility are made before leaving camp by sticking bamboo wands in the snow perpendicular to the proposed return route. The normal procedure for navigation in a whiteout, without a receiver, is to use a compass and dead reckoning. It is no easy task to travel seven to eight kilometres (close to five miles) across an almost flat icefield in zero visibility. If your navigation is accurate, you cross the icefield, hit your wands and follow them back to camp. Navigation can be so difficult that parties have been forced to spend a cold night dug into the snow while they waited for the morning sun to burn off the cloud.

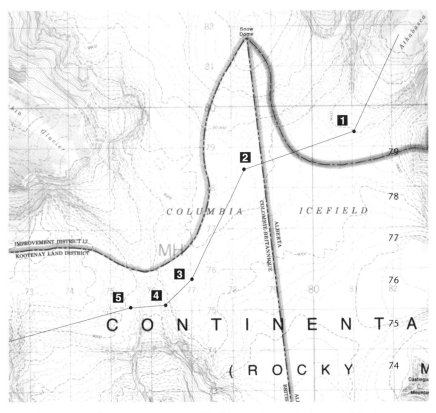

The first day of the trip, you will ski up the Athabasca Glacier to the Columbia Icefield via a snow ramp up a headwall between large crevasses and set up base camp. The camp is located where it is easy to find the top of the ramp even in poor weather. The second day you will cross the flat, featureless icefield to the base of the summit where you leave your skis and climb to the top. On the way to the peak, you have to cross a "trench," in the icefield formed where two heavily crevassed glaciers drop away on each side. In order to easily and safely cross, it is critical to find the highest point of the trench where the crevasses are the smallest. You have made the trip several times before and are intimately familiar with the way, so you do not enter waypoints in advance. However, you will store critical points during the trip to the peak just in case you need to use the receiver to retrace your steps in bad weather.

The day of the trip arrives and after a long drive you arrive at the staging area. You take a map along even though you are familiar with the route and of course you have your compass, just in case the receiver fails to perform. Before you leave your vehicle, you initialize the receiver to the following settings:

- **Map datum: North American Datum 1927 (NAD 27)**
  If your receiver splits NAD 27 into separate settings for Alaska, Canada, Central America, etc., select NAD 27-Canada, otherwise, select NAD 27.

- **Units: Metric**
  The UTM grid is based on the meter and it is easier to relate to the map if the receiver reports distances in meters, so set the receiver's units to metric.

- **Coordinate grid: UTM**

- **North setting: Magnetic North**
  A compass may be used to get between points. If the receiver is set to report bearings between points as magnetic bearings, they can be directly dialed into the compass without additional compensation for the declination.

- **CDI limit: Small**
  If the Course Deviation Indicator's tolerance is selectable, set it somewhere between 250 to 500 m. The receiver's Goto function will be used to navigate if there is bad weather. A CDI limit of 250 to 500 m means you will stray at most 250 or 500 m from course before the receiver will warn you.

- **WAAS setting: Off**
  As you are in an area where there is no WAAS coverage, turn WAAS off so as to not introduce error.

After you initialize your receiver, you return it to your backpack and clip on your skis. You do not bother to mark the car's location because there is no difficulty finding your way down the Athabasca Glacier back to the staging area even in horrible weather. You and your friends start off and in no time reach the top of the ramp at the headwall, which is the first point you need to record. You need a breather here anyway. You get the receiver out of your backpack and after it locks onto the satellites, you record the first point of the trip:

 #1   11U   481019m.E. 5779434m.N. RAMP

From the top of the ramp, you ski onto the Columbia Icefield to a flat area just south of the Snowdome. You set up camp and place a line of wands for tomorrow's trip as a safety precaution. You also record the position of your camp:

 #2   11U   478327m.E. 5778541m.N. CAMP

The rising sun finds you and your friends equipped and starting across the icefield. The weather is beautiful. As a precaution you have an extra set of batteries in your backpack. If the weather turns bad and you need to use your receiver to get back, you will have to use the energy-eating backlight. You also carry an extra bundle of wands. The receiver will get you to the best part of the trench and maybe exactly where you need to cross, but you will place wands at both ends of the trench and along the best passage to make the crossing easier in whiteout conditions. The second day of your trip is going as planned and you make rapid progress to the top of the icefield where you make a right turn to head to the trench. You take a short break and record the turning point as another waypoint:

#3   11U   477016m.E. 5775836m.N. R-TURN

Soon you reach the trench, where you spend some time finding the narrowest part. Once you find the best place, you strategically place wands and mark it as another waypoint:

#4   11U   476328m.E. 5775207m.N. TREN-E

As you cross the trench, you continue to place wands to indicate the best passage. It dawns on you that the wands increase the accuracy of the GPS receiver in the same way that Differential GPS works. When you encounter a wand, you know exactly where you are even if the receiver tells you differently. The receiver can lead you close, but the wands provide the increased accuracy necessary for a safe crossing. The important function the receiver performs is to get you close enough to the trench that you can find the wands—something you would not dare try with compass alone. Once on the other side of the trench, you record another waypoint:

#5   11U   475542m.E. 5775023m.N. TREN-W

Now both the east and west sides of the trench are marked. If a whiteout occurs, the receiver will be able to help you enter and cross the narrowest part of the trench. You have to travel 5 km (3.1 mi.) and an elevation gain of 610 m (2,001 ft.) before you reach the base, so you put the receiver away and start off again. When you reach the base of Mount Columbia, you leave your skis and mark their position:

#6   11U   470518m.E. 5774345m.N. BASE-C

You climb the last 370 m (1,214 ft.) to the summit pyramid, taking care not to fall through the double cornice on the summit ridge. At the top, you enjoy the marvelous view of the surrounding mountains, with Mount Robson a glistening white fang to the north. You take the receiver out of your backpack and mark the summit—not that you will need it for navigation, but as a memento of being at one of the most gorgeous places on earth.

You decide to make a route of the return trip, just to see the distances and bearings between the waypoints. The map shows all the waypoints except the last two. The information given from the route function is shown below. The distances are in kilometers and the bearings have a magnetic reference.

Name	Point	Desired Track	Distance km
SUMMIT off map	#7		
		69°	0.6
BASE-C off map	#6		
		63°	5.1
TREN-W	#5		
		58°	0.8
TREN-E	#4		
		29°	0.9
R-TURN	#3		
		7°	3
CAMP	#2		
		53°	2.8
RAMP	#1		

You add up the distances of the journey's legs from SUMMIT to CAMP and get 10.4 km (6.5 mi.). You do not really plan on using the route function to get back, but you never really knew the exact distance from the base camp to the peak.

When you look up from the receiver, you notice the cloud from the valley below creeping up the glacier toward the icefield. It has already filled the trench, which means it is time to get moving—fast. You put the receiver into your backpack and start down to the base with your friends. By the time you reach your skis, you are in a thick cloud and the wind is filling your upward track with blowing snow, but you are not worried. With the receiver guiding the way, it will be a record run back to camp and not a cold night out.

Once your skis are on, you pull out the receiver, get it locked on, turn on the backlight for easier reading in the poor light and press the Goto function. You need to get from the base to the west end of the trench, so you select TREN-W as the waypoint you are going to. You select the compass steering screen that reports your current heading and the necessary heading to reach the trench. It will be just like using a compass, as you have done several times in the past, but better because you will always know the correct bearing to get to your destination even if you move off course.

The steering screen shows the trench at a bearing of 63°, so you set course (track) to match the bearing.

You look at the estimated time en route (ETE) at the bottom of the screen (Time to Next). At your present speed and if you stay on course, it will take about 30 minutes to get to the trench, but you know you will have to slow down, so it will take even longer. As you cautiously ski down, you find that you can stay on course reasonably well, so you turn off the backlight and only turn it on for an occasional quick look to make sure you are still on course. It seems as though your plan to get back to camp using the receiver will work, but only if you have enough batteries. Even though you have some spares, you know you had better conserve, just to be sure. Each time you look at the steering display, if your present track does not match the correct bearing, you check the off course statistic, whether on either the compass screen or the highway steering screen to see how far off course you are.

You can see you are 72.3 m (237.2 ft.) to the right of the direct line to TREN-W and the highway is pointing to the left telling you to steer left to get on course. You are ecstatic because, before owning a receiver, you have never stayed so close to the correct bearing in a whiteout, and better than staying on the correct bearing, you also know exactly how far you have strayed and what to do to get back on course. You adjust your track to 63°, which is 22° to the left, and continue on.

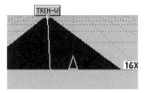

The next time you look at the receiver, you notice you have strayed again, but this time you are to the left of the direct course by 34.9 m (114.5 ft.).

As you have been off course for a while, the bearing to TREN-W has changed from 63° to 64°, so you steer slightly to the right to follow the new bearing. You change to the compass screen and see that it is just over 2.4 km (1.5 mi) to the trench—something you would have never known without a GPS receiver. You press on, making occasional course adjustments until

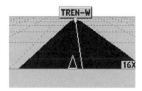

trench

finally, two hours after leaving the base of Mount Columbia, you arrive at the west end of the trench and find your wands.

You turn the receiver off while you rope in and prepare to cross. When you are ready to go, you turn the receiver on and activate the Goto function. You select the TREN-E waypoint. The steering screen shows the bearing to be 58°, so you leave the receiver on and watch the screen as you adjust your course to match. As you enter the trench, your pace really slows and you notice the receiver no longer gives you an ETE, but you know it can still accurately calculate the bearing from your present position to the other side of the trench. This juncture is critical, so you leave the backlight on and watch the screen continuously all while feeling for wands. Occasionally you check the map screen to verify your overall position in the trench, and your course.

The first time you check the receiver's map, you see you are slightly to the left of the direct course. You also notice the bearing to TREN-E has changed to 59°. You have strayed slightly, so you adjust your track to the new bearing of 59°. When you hit your first line of wands, your confidence in the receiver increases. After traveling a short while, you check the map screen to see you have veered from the left of the straight course to the right.

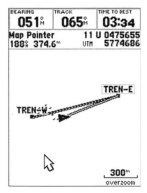

You quickly change to the highway steering screen and see that you are off course to the right by 67.2 m (220.5 ft.).

Mt. Columbia

You are farther off course than you like or need to be and part of the problem is your own lack of vigilance. The bearing to the end of the trench is now 45°, so you watch the receiver more closely. A slow hour later, you find all the wands you placed and the receiver's map indicates you have successfully made it through the trench to the TREN-E waypoint.

This is a first. You have never gotten so far in such poor visibility and you would not have been able to do it without the combination of the receiver and wands. Now it is nearly a straight shot back to camp. You take off your ropes and activate the Goto function to lead you to R-TURN. The steering screen responds to your request and shows the bearing to be 29°. You start off, keeping an eye on the receiver.

Your vigilance on the leg to R-TURN results in a relatively quick trip of 40 minutes. After resting, you change the batteries and activate the Goto function to lead you to CAMP. Watching the receiver you adjust your track to 7°. The receiver calculates an ETE of approximately one hour at your present speed. With a bit of weaving back and forth to stay on track, you hit your wands an hour and 15 minutes later. Yeah! It is going to be a warm night. You follow the wands back to camp and as you unzip the flap to your tent, you discover someone else is already in it! They hit your wands and are taking refuge from the weather in your camp. You make a note in your journal: "Bring extra receivers to sell at the staging area."

8 Latitude, Longitude and a Kayaking Trip

The Latitude/Longitude Grid

The latitude/longitude grid is familiar to most people. It is printed on almost all maps even if it is not the primary grid. If you travel in a part of the world where your receiver does not have the local grid, do not worry because the map probably has latitude and longitude. The latitude/longitude grid is based on a sphere. The figure shows how the globe is divided by the lines of latitude and longitude.

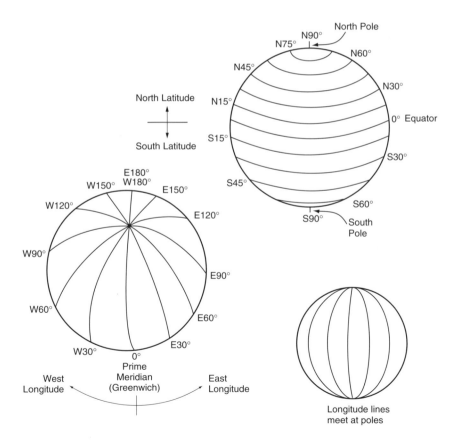

Lines of latitude go around the world parallel to the equator. Lines of longitude go from pole to pole. On a map, latitude lines are horizontal and longitude lines are vertical. If you need a review of degrees, minutes and seconds and how they relate to each other, turn to Chapter 17. Here are some interesting facts about latitude and longitude:

Latitude

- Lines parallel to the equator.
- Hemispheres designated North (N) and South (S).
    Equator is 0°.
    North pole is N 90°.
    South pole is S 90°.
- May be expressed in three formats.
    Hemisphere degrees minutes seconds: S 38° 27' 54".
    Hemisphere degrees minutes: N 23° 27.3'.
    Hemisphere degrees: N 58.385°.
- 1° of latitude is 111.12 km (69.05 mi.).
- 1' is one nautical mile (1.85 km, 1.15 mi.).

Longitude

- Lines run from pole to pole.
- Greenwich, England is the Prime Meridian.
- Hemispheres designated West (W) and East (E) of the Prime Meridian.
    Prime Meridian is 0°.
    International Date Line is W 180° (same as E 180°).
- May be expressed in three formats.
    Hemisphere degrees minutes seconds: E 140° 54' 09".
    Hemisphere degrees minutes: W 67° 28.75'.
    Hemisphere degrees: E 86.824°.
- Longitude lines converge at the poles.
- 1° of longitude is 111.12 km (69.05 mi.) only at the equator.
- 1' is not one nautical mile except at the equator.

Latitude and Longitude Coordinates

- Coordinate usually written hemisphere latitude, hemisphere longitude.
- N 47° 19.56', E 102° 42.84'.
- Called geographic coordinate because it is based on a sphere.

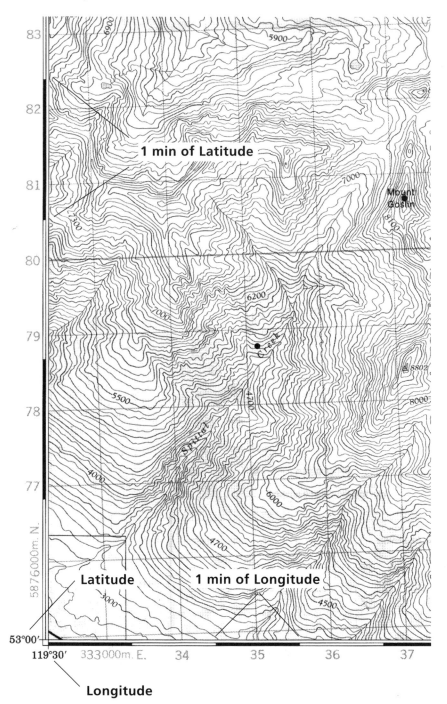

Finding the Latitude/Longitude Grid on Maps

Some maps make it easy to use the latitude/longitude grid. The map shown, a product of Natural Resources Canada, is the southwest corner of the Mount Robson, British Columbia, Canada topographical map. It has a 1 minute latitude/longitude grid.

The starting coordinates are shown in the bottom left corner. For this map, the latitude is N 53° 00' while the longitude is W 119° 30'. From the corner, the latitude/longitude grid is marked off in one minute intervals as indicated by the alternating black and white lines printed on the map's edges. The blue numbers correspond to the UTM grid and have nothing to do with finding latitude/longitude coordinates. Up the left side of the map, the end of the white line, just below the 77 of the UTM grid, represents the latitude N 53° 01'. The end of the black mark above that is N 53° 02' and so forth. The longitude is measured the same way, but the minutes decrease as you travel east toward the prime meridian. The end of first black line at the bottom of the page is W 119° 29', the end of the next white line is W 119° 28, etc. For either latitude or longitude, one half of the alternating lines is half of a minute, one quarter is a quarter of a minute, etc. To get the coordinate of a location, place a ruler perpendicular to the side of the map for latitude or to the bottom for longitude and measure to the closest tenth of a minute. Do not be confused by the UTM grid, which is printed on the map, just ignore it. Two examples of coordinates taken from the map on the previous page are:

- Mount Goslin:
  N 53° 3.2' W 119° 25.7'
- The letter "C" in Spittal Creek:
  N 53° 2.0' W 119° 27.4'

It is possible to measure coordinates with your eyes alone on a map with such clear, easy-to-use systems such as the one shown in the picture. Other types of maps require some preparation to use the latitude/longitude grid. How to do this is explained on the next page.

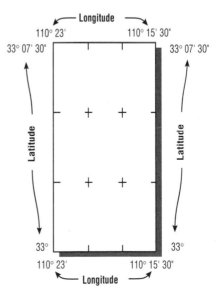

A USGS map before drawing latitude/longitude grid.

Preparing USGS 7.5' Maps

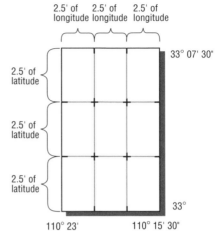

The 7.5' topographical maps printed by the US Geological Survey require some preparation when using the latitude/longitude grid. Tick marks on the side of the map and crosses inside the map, as shown in the figure, divide the maps into 2.5' rectangles. To draw the grid, use a ruler to draw from one side of the map through the crosses to the other side. A subdivided map appears similar to the figure.

A USGS map after drawing the latitude and longitude grid.

A 2.5' rectangle of the southwest corner of the USGS Burrows Lake, Wisconsin topographical map on the next page demonstrates that an area 2.5' x 2.5' is much too large to accurately read a coordinate without taking further steps. Using your eyes alone, try to find the coordinate of the island in the southern part of Burrows Lake—labeled #1.

The longitude is just over half way between W 89° 50' 00" and W 89° 52' 30", which makes it about W 89° 51' 15". The latitude is about one fifth of the way between N 45° 37' 30" and N 45° 40' 00", which gives it a latitude about N 45° 38' 00". The island's actual coordinate is N 45° 37' 55" W 89° 51' 23", which means visual measurement differed from the true coordinate by 8" in longitude and 5" in latitude. An error of 5" in latitude equates to 0.083', which is the same as 0.083 nautical miles or 506.34 ft. (154.3 m). The 8" error in longitude does not directly correlate to nautical miles since it is not at the equator, but the distance scale at the bottom of the map reveals that 2.5' of longitude at this latitude is 2 statute miles. Once all the conversions are done, 8" in longitude on this map is an error of 563.2 ft. (171.6 m). The error was not really that bad for an eyeball only measurement, but it is much easier to use latitude/longitude on a USGS 7.5' map if the 2.5' grid is further subdivided.

There are two easy methods to subdivide any latitude/longitude grid that is too large for convenient use. The first is to use an ordinary ruler and a pencil to draw more lines between the main latitude/longitude lines, which in this case are the 2.5' lines. The second is to use a special ruler that is calibrated to minutes and seconds to directly read coordinates from the 2.5' by 2.5' rectangles. Both methods will be illustrated.

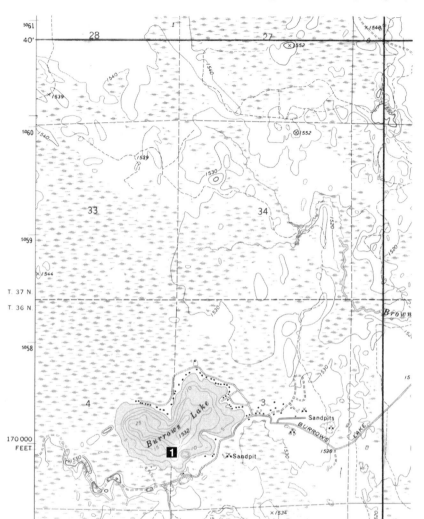

A 2.5' area on USGS Burrows Lake, Wisconsin map (1:24,000 scale).

Drawing a Finer Grid

The key to subdividing a grid is to divide it by a number that results in a fraction that is easy to add in your head. It is easy to divide any grid into 4 equal parts, but in the case of a USGS 7.5' map, dividing the 2.5' rectangle by 4 means that each subdivision is 0.625' or 37.5" wide. It is not easy to perform mental calculations with units of 0.625, so the grid needs to be divided more sensibly. The 2.5' grid is best divided by either 5, which results in subdivisions of 0.5' each, or 10, which provides 0.25' between lines. It is easiest to work with 0.5' intervals because there are fewer lines to draw, so 5 is probably the best divisor to use. The southeast corner of USGS Burrows Lake is shown with the 2.5' rectangle subdivided into 5 equal parts in both latitude and longitude.

The finer grid makes it much easier to find latitude/longitude coordinates to the tenth of a minute. For example, using the map on the next page, the "S" in the northern part of Swamp Creek, label #1 on the map, has a latitude that is two-fifths of the way between N 45° 39.5' and N 45° 40', which is N 45° 39.7', and a longitude four-fifths of the way between W 89° 46.5' and W 89° 47', which is W 89° 46.9'. The exact coordinate for point #1 is N 45° 39.63' W 89° 46.85'. The resulting error in latitude is 0.07' (4.2") or about 425.3 ft. (129.6 m) and the error in the longitude measurement is 0.05' (3"), which for the latitude of this map equates to about 211.2 ft. (64.4 m). The measurement is only slightly more accurate than the example of Burrows Lake where only the 2.5' grid was used, but the finer grid used in this example makes it much easier to accurately and quickly find a coordinate using the eye alone. The exact coordinates of the four locations marked on the map are given below. See how close you can come to getting the same coordinate without using a ruler.

Point	Latitude	Longitude
#1	N 45° 39.63'	W 89° 46.85'
#2	N 45° 38.68'	W 89° 47.16'
#3	N 45° 37.83'	W 89° 46.11'
#4	N 45° 39.36'	W 89° 45.66'

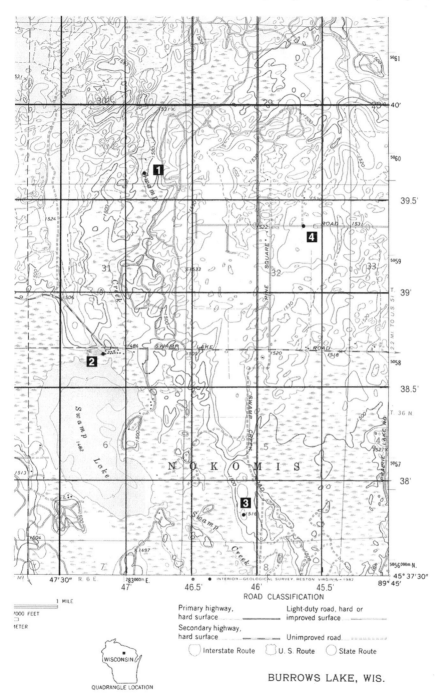

BURROWS LAKE, WIS.

QUADRANGLE LOCATION

ROAD CLASSIFICATION

Primary highway,
hard surface ————— Light-duty road, hard or improved surface

Secondary highway,
hard surface ————— Unimproved road

◯ Interstate Route ◯ U. S. Route ◯ State Route

WISCONSIN

1 MILE
7000 FEET
1ETER

Using a Minute/Second Calibrated Ruler

The easiest and most accurate way to measure latitude/longitude is to use a minute/second calibrated ruler. It provides a method to measure coordinates to an accuracy of about 1" on a 1:24,000 scale map, which translates to an accuracy of approximately 30.9 m (101.3 ft.) or better and the time it takes to prepare the map is minimal. On a USGS 7.5' map, using a minute/second calibrated ruler requires that you draw only the lines for the 2.5' rectangles as described earlier. The ruler does the additional subdividing to make reading coordinates simple and accurate. An example of such a ruler is the Topo Companion shown here. You can also make your own minute/second calibrated rulers as shown in Chapter 9.

   The numbers along the bottom of the rulers correspond to map scales: 1:24,000, 1:25,000, 1:50,000, 1:63,360 and 1:250,000. The USGS 7.5' topographical maps use the 1:24,000 scale on the minute/second calibrated ruler. The numbers on the 1/24K of the ruler represent tens of seconds while the lines between the numbers are individual seconds. How the numbers correspond to the 2.5' rectangle is shown in the figure. The ruler measures a full minute whenever it starts at a given number and ends on a number of the same value. The figure shows a full minute from 00 to 00 or 30 to 30. However, a full minute is also traversed going from 10 to 10, or 20 to 20 and so forth.

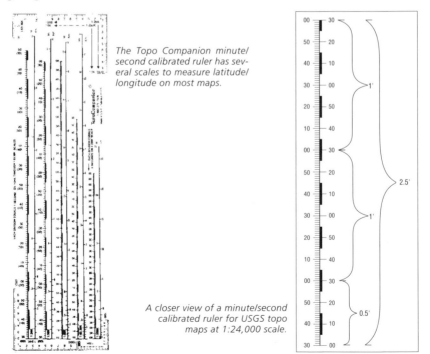

The Topo Companion minute/second calibrated ruler has several scales to measure latitude/longitude on most maps.

A closer view of a minute/second calibrated ruler for USGS topo maps at 1:24,000 scale.

Note the ruler starts at the bottom with 30 on the left and 00 on the right. The latitude or longitude of a 2.5' rectangle can start with either 00" or 30". The latitude of the southeast corner of the USGS Burrows Lake is N 45° 37' 30" while the longitude is W 89° 45' 00" (the 00" is not printed on the map, but it is shown here to demonstrate that it corresponds to the 00 on the minute/second calibrated ruler). If the coordinate ends in 30", use the numbers that start at 30 in your measurement. If the coordinate starts at 00", or if the seconds are omitted because they are zero, use the numbers that start with 00.

The key to using a minute/second calibrated ruler is to place the ends of the scale on adjacent latitude or longitude lines, then count off the seconds to the location. The map shown in the figure is the northeast corner of the USGS Four Peaks, Arizona map.

The horizontally and vertically drawn lines along with the top and right side of the map form the 2.5' rectangle. To measure latitude, one end of the ruler touches the bottom of the 2.5' rectangle while the other end touches the top. From the bottom of the ruler, count up the seconds to the location of Three Bar Cabin. The latitude of the bottom of the 2.5' rectangle is N 33° 42' 30", so use the numbers on the left of the scale that start with 30. The numbers on the left side of the scale and how they correspond to a latitude coordinate are given below:

Number on scale		Corresponding latitude
30	→	N 33° 42' 30"
40	→	N 33° 42' 40"
50	→	N 33° 42' 50"
00	›	N 33° 43' 00"
10	→	N 33° 43' 10"

Three Bar Cabin lies above 00, but below 10, so its latitude coordinate is between N 33° 43' 00" and N 33° 43' 10". The small tick lines between 00 and 10 must be counted to get to the exact coordinate. The cabin lies directly across from the ninth tick mark, so the final latitude coordinate is N 33° 43' 09".

It is just as easy to measure the longitude coordinate. The figure on the next page shows how the ends of the ruler are placed on the longitude lines of the 2.5' rectangle. Notice that the ruler is not completely horizontal because only at the equator is 2.5' of latitude the same physical distance as 2.5' of longitude. However, even though the ruler is at an angle, if the ends of the scale are on the longitude lines, the measurement will be accurate. Remember, the ruler measures minutes

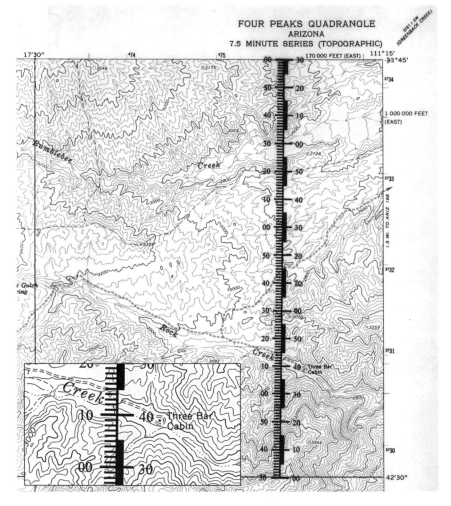

and seconds, not distance, so the spacing between the longitude lines is unimportant. The only requirement for the ruler to work on any scale is that the number of minutes and seconds between adjacent latitude and longitude lines is the same. In this case, there are 2.5' between the latitude lines and the same amount between the longitude lines.

From the right-hand end of the ruler, count up the minutes and seconds to the point directly above Three Bar Cabin. The coordinate of the longitude line on the right of the 2.5' rectangle is W 111° 15', so use the numbers on the right, or in this position the top, of the scale because they start with 00. The relationship between the numbers on the scale and the corresponding longitude coordinate is given on the next page.

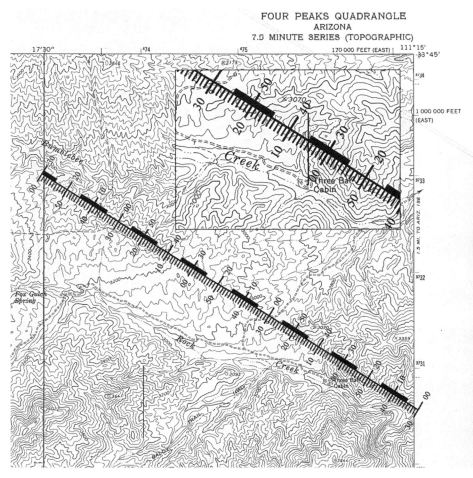

Number on scale		Corresponding latitude
00	→	W 111° 15' 00"
10	→	W 111° 15' 10"
20	→	W 111° 15' 20"
30	→	W 111° 15' 30"
40	→	W 111° 15' 40"

The location of Three Bar Cabin lies between 30 and 40 on the scale, which translates to a coordinate between W 111° 15' 30" and W 111° 15' 40". Count the small tick marks between 30 and 40 to get the exact coordinate of W 111° 15' 35". The final coordinate for Three Bar Cabin in latitude/longitude is

N 33° 43' 09", W 111° 15' 35"

A Kayak Trip

In May, your brother is coming to visit you in Dupont, Alaska and really wants to go to your cabin. When you describe how beautiful and peaceful it is there, he decides he wants to go as soon as he arrives and stay for the entire three days he will be in town. The only transportation you have between your house and the cabin is a kayak. It is only a 10.8 mi. (17.4 km) paddle, but your brother's plane arrives in Juneau at 10:30 pm and it will be dark before you can even start the trip. It is easy to navigate to the cabin by sight during the day and in the dark it is still possible, but much more difficult.

You decide your GPS receiver can guide you directly to the cabin, even in the dark, if you set it up so the navigation screens are continuously visible. It is impossible to hold the receiver and paddle at the same time, so you mount the receiver to the kayak. Another problem you need to overcome is powering the receiver. You will make the trip in the dark and will need the receiver's backlight continuously illuminated so you can see the screen. The backlight uses a lot of power, which means a lot of batteries, but you also need to attach lights to the kayak to be able to make it safely through the busy traffic of Stephens Passage. The lights are powered by a motorcycle battery and a quick look at the receiver's manual reveals that the battery's voltage lies in an acceptable range, so the battery will power both the receiver and the lights. You decide to use the Route function to automatically guide you from one waypoint to the next without touching any buttons, thereby leaving your hands free to paddle.

Using your minute/second calibrated ruler, you measure the latitude/longitude coordinates for the trip's waypoints from the USGS Juneau, Alaska (A-1) map shown on the next page. The map is from the USGS 15' series and has a scale of 1:63,360. The latitude/longitude grid on the map forms 5' rectangles instead of the 2.5' rectangles of the 7.5' maps described above. The minute/second calibrated ruler is used in exactly the same way as demonstrated previously except you need to use the 1:63,360 scale to make the measurements.

The coordinates and names of the five waypoints are shown on the map:

Point	Latitude	Longitude	Name
#1	N 58° 13' 45"	W 134° 15' 55"	DUPONT
#2	N 58° 11' 53"	W 134° 14' 20"	TANTAL
#3	N 58° 08' 40"	W 134° 19' 45"	OLIVER
#4	N 58° 06' 35"	W 134° 18' 35"	P-TAGE
#5	N 58° 05' 50"	W 134° 18' 47"	ACABIN

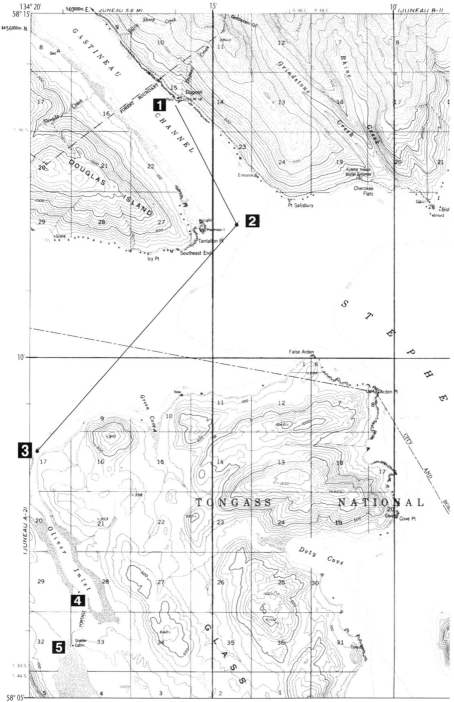

USGS Juneau, Alaska (A-1) (1:63,360 scale).

Before entering the coordinates into your receiver, set it to the proper settings:

- **Map datum: North American Datum 1927 (NAD 27)**
  If your receiver splits NAD 27 into separate settings for Alaska, Canada, Central America, etc., select NAD 27-Alaska, otherwise, select NAD 27.

- **Units: Statute**
  Nautical units are best suited for latitude/longitude coordinates, but you have never used them before and can not relate to a nautical mile, so use statute.

- **Coordinate grid: Latitude/Longitude**
  Select the degrees, minutes and seconds format to correspond to the coordinates measured off the map.

- **North setting: True North**
  A compass is not going to be used to navigate, so it does not really matter if the receiver's bearings are oriented to the magnetic or north pole. You arbitrarily decide to make the bearings relate to the map and select the True North mode.

- **CDI limit: Small**
  If the Course Deviation Indicator's tolerance is selectable, set it somewhere between 0.25 and 0.5 mi. On the water, there are no obstacles in the route you have planned, so a small CDI will allow the highway navigation screen to keep you on course.

- **WAAS setting: On**
  As you are in an area where there is WAAS coverage, turn WAAS on for increased accuracy.

Once the waypoints are in the receiver's memory, you set up the route that will lead you from DUPONT through all the intervening waypoints until you arrive at the cabin. The distance is expressed in statute miles and the bearings relate to true north as set above.

Name	Point	Desired Track	Distance mi
DUPONT	#1		
		156°	2.4
TANTAL	#2		
		222°	5.0
OLIVER	#3		
		164°	2.5
P-TAGE	#4		
		188°	0.9
ACABIN	#5		

The plan to navigate the 10.8 mi. (17.4 km) is simple: use the receiver's Route function to guide you the entire trip. You will paddle the kayak from DUPONT to P-TAGE where you will portage the kayak the remaining 0.9 mi. (1.45 km) to the cabin. While you are in the kayak and the receiver is connected to the battery, you will have access to the steering screens and other navigational statistics like speed, bearing, estimated time en route, etc. Your receiver uses averaging and smoothing algorithms, so even at your slow speed the navigational statistics will be meaningful. You will also take a compass and a map, but if something were to happen to the receiver, you would use the compass to paddle due south to land, then either slowly follow the coastline west to Oliver Inlet or wait for sunrise to easily complete the trip.

The day finally arrives. Your brother's plane pulls in at 10:40 pm and after several delays it is not until midnight that you are ready to shove off in the kayak. Before paddling, you turn on the lights and the receiver. Once the receiver is locked onto the satellites, you activate the route that leads to the cabin. The receiver instantly detects that you are already at the route's first waypoint, so it immediately starts pointing to the next waypoint, which is TANTAL.

After paddling about halfway to TANTAL, you switch to the highway navigation screen and notice that you are slightly off course to the left of where you should be. You had been traveling at a bearing of 154° when it should have been 156°; as a result, you are off course to the left, or in other words you have a CrossTrack Error, of 264 ft. (80.5 m), which is not bad, but you also notice the bearing to TANTAL has changed from the 156° it was originally to 159°. You do not really want to steer deeper into Stephens Passage, so you adjust your track to 159° and continue. As you hold your course, you notice the CrossTrack Error steadily decreases as your position slowly returns to the center line of the road as shown on the highway screen. The receiver advises you of your arrival at TANTAL, then automatically switches and starts steering you across Stephens Passage to Oliver Inlet. You adjust your course to the new bearing of 222°.

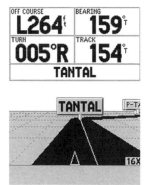

As you paddle along, you and your brother get talking and you do not pay attention to the receiver. When you do look up, you see you have gone almost 0.6 mi. (0.97 km) at a bearing of 252°. The arrow on the compass navigation screen points to the left and the bearing to OLIVER is now 218°.

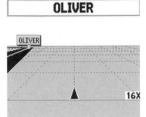

You switch to the highway screen. The direction of the highway also off to the left indicating you need to steer left to get back on course. It also shows your CrossTrack Error to be 0.32 mi. (1689.6 ft. or 515 m) to the right of the intended course.

You decide to try an experiment to get back to the direct line between TANTAL and OLIVER as fast as possible. The figure illustrates your position at the X. The direct course between TANTAL and OLIVER is 222°, but because you paddled on a bearing of 252°, you are 0.32 mi. away from the direct line course as indicated by the CrossTrack Error. The fastest way to return to the direct line is to follow the route indicated by the dotted line, which is perpendicular to the direct route. The dotted line bearing is

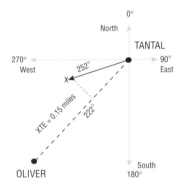

$$222° - 90° = 132°$$

You turn the kayak to the left until your bearing is 132° and paddle until your CrossTrack Error is zero. Soon you are back on the direct route and turn right to a bearing of 222° to head straight to OLIVER. Everything is smooth sailing without much traffic until you get halfway into Stephens Passage where you hear the loud sound of a fast motorboat. Fortunately they see you and give you plenty of room, but when the sound of the motor dies down, you hear something that sounds like a dog barking. No dog on land could sound that close, so you decide to investigate.

Before you start paddling toward the dog's bark, you activate the Man-Overboard (MOB) function, which immediately marks your present position. You plan to investigate the sound, then return to where you are right now to continue the trip to Oliver Inlet. The MOB function not only marks your current position, but it automatically activates the Goto function and steers you to the position just marked. While you are looking for the dog, you will ignore the receiver's screen. When you are ready to continue your trip, the receiver will lead you back to the MOB coordinate where you will disengage the Goto function and resume the route to the cabin. Out of curiosity you switch to the map screen and see that the MOB waypoint is about halfway between TANTAL and OLIVER.

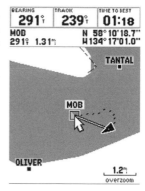

Because you are following the dog's bark and not the receiver, you leave it on the map screen just to see where you are going in relation to the waypoints that lead to the cabin. Either the dog is afraid of you and is swimming away or you are having a hard time following the sound as it travels over the water because the receiver's map shows you paddling all over the place.

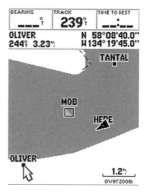

Sure enough, the dog is not on land and as you pull it on board, it seems really happy to see you. When you notice it does not have any tags, you are pretty sure the owners will not even know where to begin to look for their lost pet. You take another look at the receiver's map. You first check to make sure the map is pointing north up so everything looks like the map you used to plan the trip. If you return to the MOB waypoint, it will take a lot of extra paddling because the dog was so far away. You decide the best approach is to paddle directly from your present position to OLIVER, so you cancel the MOB Goto function. The method you use to continue your journey depends on your receiver. On some receivers you can simply activate the original route you were following. The receiver knows you are past TANTAL and will automatically begin to steer you to OLIVER. If your receiver does not have that capability, you can save your current position as the HERE waypoint and form a new route from HERE to OLIVER to P-TAGE, then finally to ACABIN.

Your receiver cannot pick up a route where it left off, so you store your position as HERE.

Using the new waypoint, you form a new route.

Name	Point	Desired Track	Distance mi
HERE			
		244°	3.2
OLIVER	#3		
		164°	2.5
P-TAGE	#4		
		188°	0.9
ACABIN	#5		

From where you are right now, it is still 6.6 mi. (10.6 km) to the cabin. You activate the new route, switch to the steering screen and swing the kayak around to a bearing of 244°. The trip continues with few course corrections until you arrive at the cabin.

Three glorious days later, when it is time to go home, it is easy to get the receiver ready for the trip back because you only have to press a single button to reverse the original route. When you told the receiver to reverse the route, it automatically formed the route shown below:

Name	Point	Desired Track	Distance mi
ACABIN	#5		
		8°	0.9
P-TAGE	#4		
		344°	2.5
OLIVER	#3		
		42°	5.0
TANTAL	#2		
		336°	2.4
DUPONT	#1		

Once more, in the dark with the receiver showing the way, you, your brother and new dog paddle from the cabin back to the house glad you were able to spend as much time there as you did.

9 More Latitude, Longitude and a Sailboat Rally

Every year, your sailing club has a timed race where the object is not to be the fastest, but the closest to a set time between points. The time is fixed to teach you how to better control the boat and you are docked points for every minute you are too fast or too slow. Points are also given for the proximity you arrive at each location. Some of the places are fairly remote and it would be difficult for judges to monitor a boat's arrival, so each crew is given an Instamatic camera to prove how close they got to each marker.

It is your fifth year in the race. You finally understand how to handle the craft and can sail proficiently in most conditions, but you are hopelessly inept at judging your speed in the water. Last year, you zoomed as fast as you could to get close to each point, then waited until the time was almost up before moving in the last little bit. Your method left a lot to be desired because you placed 45th out of 100 contestants. This year you need to be a bit more controlled. You search the rules carefully and find there are no restrictions on GPS receivers. You outfit your boat with an external antenna, power cord and mounting hardware because you plan to use the receiver's navigational statistics to help you arrive right on time.

The stopping points of the race have been published on the official chart, so you reach for your ruler to measure coordinates for your route. The coordinate grid on the chart is latitude/longitude, so you grab your minute/second calibrated ruler to start measuring, but none of the scales seem to work. You notice the scale at the bottom of the map: 1:40,000.

"Great!" you complain. The ruler you have does not have the scale you need. Then you notice the subdivided lines that have "LATITUDE" and "LONGITUDE" written above them. After comparing the lengths of the

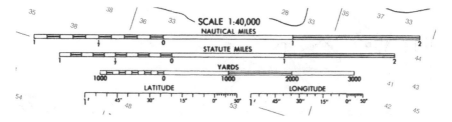

scales to the distance between the latitude and longitude grid lines, you realize that you can make your own minute/second calibrated ruler for the 1:40,000 scale. There are three ways to make the ruler:

1. Make one ruler, based on the latitude grid line, and use it with any 1:40,000 scale map exactly like the Topo Companion ruler described in Chapter 8.
2. Make two rulers: one for latitude and the other for longitude. They would be different lengths and would not be interchangeable.
3. Make a ruler with longitude on the left side and latitude along the top as shown in the figure. This type of ruler makes it possible to place the ruler's corner on an object and easily read the coordinates. However, it can only be used with this map.

You decide to make a ruler like the one described in the third option above. To make the ruler, first measure the distance between two latitude lines. For this chart at this scale, the distance is 9.2 cm (3.62 in.). Use centimeters because it is much easier to divide a length that is based on a factor of 10. Inches are subdivided into 1/4, 1/16 or 1/32 increments, which result in difficult math when dividing. Draw a vertical line 9.2 cm long on a piece of paper. Because the latitude lines are 2' apart, the line represents 2' of latitude. Label the bottom of the line 2' as shown in the figure. Measure down from the top 4.6 cm, or halfway down, draw another line and label it 1'. The top of the line represents 0', but do not label it because it will get in the way of the longitude line when it is drawn later. There is enough room between each minute mark to make 10 subdivisions, which translate into 0.1' marks. The ruler shown in the figure has 0.1' subdivisions, but only every other mark is labeled so the ruler does not look cluttered.

Dividing each minute into 10 equal units translates to 0.46 cm between each line. To do the subdivision, place the top of the ruler at the top of the line. Measure down 0.46 cm and draw the first small line. Measure down an additional 0.46 cm, to 0.92 cm, and draw the second line, which can be labeled 0.2'. Continue down the ruler in 0.46 cm increments until the subdivisions are drawn and labeled as

Custom-made ruler for a 1:40,000 scale chart.

shown in the figure. The ruler in its present form is equivalent to a Topo Companion ruler and can be used as shown earlier. But because you chose the option 3 ruler, you need to add the longitude scale.

Back on the chart, the ruler measures 7 cm (2.76 in.) between adjacent longitude lines. On the paper you are using to make the ruler, draw a 7 cm horizontal line to the right from the top of the vertical latitude line forming a right angle. Just as with the latitude, the longitude grid lines are separated by 2'. Label the end of the line 2' and draw a line at the halfway mark, 3.5 cm, and label it 1'. The space between the minute lines can again be subdivided into 10 equal parts to provide 0.1' marks. Only 3.5 cm separate the longitude minute marks, so each 0.1' mark is separated by only 0.35 cm. To draw the subdivisions, place the ruler at the left end of the line. Move to the right 0.35 cm, draw a short line. Move right an additional 0.35 cm, to 0.7 cm, draw a short line and label it 0.2'. Continue moving right by 0.35 cm, drawing and labeling lines until your ruler looks like the one in the figure. Once you have drawn the ruler, copy it onto a transparency so the map's features are visible when you use the scale to measure.

Measuring coordinates is easy with the ruler. The way the ruler is drawn requires the latitude scale to always be on the left and the longitude on top. To measure a coordinate, place the corner of the ruler on the location and note where the latitude and longitude lines intersect the scales. Finding the coordinate to the mouth of Howells Creek is shown in the figure.

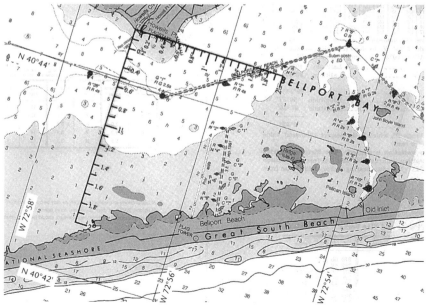

US NOAA, Long Island Intra Coastal Waterway (1: 40,000 scale).

The ruler's corner is placed at the river's mouth. The N 40° 44' latitude line intersects the latitude scale (vertical) at 0.5'. The latitude is calculated by adding the number where the latitude grid line intersects the ruler to the grid line's coordinate value, so in this case the latitude becomes:

- N 40° 44' + 0.5' = N 40° 44.5'

The same approach is used with the longitude. The W 72° 56' longitude line intersects the longitude scale between the 1.2' and 1.3' marks. Use your eye to estimate the distance between the two marks to arrive at the number 1.23'. Add the number from the scale to the value of the longitude line to get:

- W 72° 56' + 1.23' = W 72° 57.23'

The final coordinate to the mouth of Howells Creek is:

- N 40° 44.5', W 72° 57.23'

Now it is easy to measure coordinates from the map, so you begin your work. This year's contest has four locations numbered 1 through 4.

A quick look reveals that the path from #1 to #2, #2 to #3 and #4 back to #1 are not straight lines. The receiver's Estimated Time En route (ETE) calculation is based on the Velocity Made Good (VMG) measurement. Refer to Chapter 4 for an explanation of VMG and Speed Over Ground (SOG). If you are headed directly for a waypoint, the ETE is the actual time it will take to get there. If you are off course or the course is not a straight line, the VMG and ETE both vary widely. The only straight shot on the sailing course is between #3 and #4, so you break up the route between each location into a series of straight lines. You will use the receiver's Route function to lead you from one waypoint to the next and if you stay on course, the ETE will be the actual time between each point and you can use it to help meet the time requirements. You label the intermediate waypoints: 1A, 1B, 2A, 2B and 4A.

The coordinates of all the waypoints you will use along with their names are listed below.

Point	Latitude	Longitude	Name
#1	N 40° 42.38'	W 73° 13.2'	P1
#1A	N 40° 39.22'	W 73° 12.6'	P1A
#1B	N 40° 38.71'	W 73° 11.2'	P1B
#2	N 40° 38.46'	W 73° 11.43'	P2
#2A	N 40° 39.2'	W 73° 10'	P2A
#2B	N 40° 39.73'	W 73° 10'	P2B
#3	N 40° 39.57'	W 73° 10.55'	P3
#4	N 40° 42.05'	W 73° 10.68'	P4
#4A	N 40° 41.6'	W 73° 12.2'	P4A

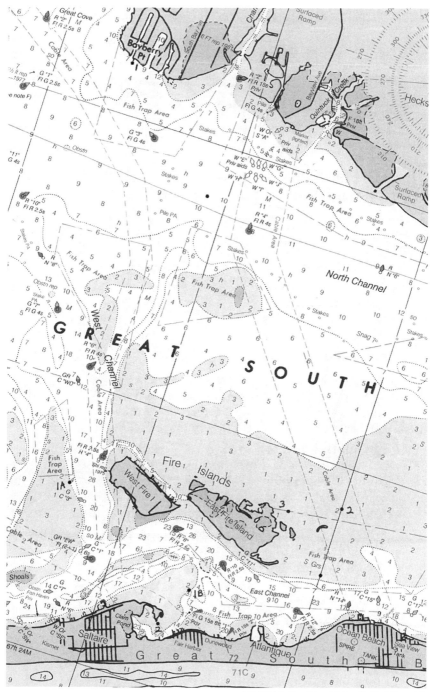

US NOAA, Fire Island Inlet (1:40,000 scale).

Before you enter the waypoints into the receiver, you need to specify the map datum. You search the official race chart in vain, but the datum was not included. You debate what to do. Never before have you had to know the datum for the race because navigation with a compass does not require it. If you ask the rally organizers, they will be suspicious and ask why you need it. You are not a very good liar, so you decide you will have to make an educated guess. The chart was made in the U.S., so the datum is probably NAD 27, NAD 83 or WGS 84. If you pick the wrong datum, the position error will only be a few meters. This will not pose a problem because you only have to get close to each point, not exactly on top of it. You decide to use NAD 27 because it is the datum used by most of the charts you own. Some of the newer charts use NAD 83, but you cannot tell from the copy if it is old or new. You set your receiver as shown below:

- **Map datum: North American Datum 1927 (NAD 27)**
  If your receiver splits NAD 27 into separate settings for Alaska, Canada, Central America, etc., select NAD 27-CONUS, otherwise, select NAD 27.

- **Units: Nautical**
  You have quite a bit of experience with charts and have a feel for nautical miles, so select nautical units.

- **Coordinate grid: Latitude/Longitude**

- **North setting: Magnetic North**
  The big, on-board compass is like an old friend and even though you are using a GPS receiver, you will turn to your own compass when actually trying to maintain a course.

- **CDI limit: A medium setting**
  You are proficient at holding an accurate course. The highway navigation screen may prove useful, so you do not want a CDI limit that is so large that it is meaningless, or one that is so small that you can never hold the course. Your receiver has a setting of 0.25, 1.25 and 5.0, so select 1.25 nautical miles.

- **WAAS setting: On**
  As you are in an area where there is WAAS coverage, turn WAAS on for increased accuracy.

After setting the receiver, you enter the waypoints and then form a route.

Name	Point	Desired Track	Distance n mi
P1	#1		
		186°	3.2
P1A	#1A		
		129°	1.2
P1B	#1B		
		229°	0.3
P2	#2		
		69°	1.3
P2A	#2A		
		14°	0.5
P2B	#2B		
		263°	0.4
P3	#3		
		11°	2.5
P4	#4		
		262°	1.2
P4A	#4A		
		330°	1.1
P1	#1		

The total trip is 11.7 nautical miles (13.5 statute miles, 21.7 km). The time for each leg was also sent with the chart, so you quickly form a table listing times and distances, and you calculate the constant speed required to cover each leg in the specified time.

Leg	Time min	Distance n mi	Speed knots
#1 to #2	36	4.7	7.8
#2 to #3	21	2.2	6.3
#3 to #4	13	2.5	11.5
#4 to #1	24	2.3	5.8

You can easily sustain the 11.5 knots needed for the jaunt between #3 and #4, so none of the legs appear to be excessively fast. Next you calculate the time that can be spent on each leg as you defined them on the map. You decide that last year's strategy still has merit, but this year you will not rush so fast then wait so long. You form the following table:

Leg	Distance n mi	Target Time min	Speed Required knots
P1 to P1A	3.2	23	8.3
P1A to P1B	1.2	8	9
P1B to P2	0.3	5	3.6
P2 to P2A	1.3	11	7.1
P2A to P2B	0.5	4	7.5
P2B to P3	0.4	6	4
P3 to P4	2.5	13	11.5
P4 to P4A	1.2	11	6.5
P4A to P1	1.1	13	5.1

Fortunately you do not have to sail the craft solo. You will stay at the helm, keep an eye on the instruments including the GPS receiver and tell the crew members what to do to keep on course and on schedule. You plan to use the Estimated Time En route (ETE) timer on the receiver to calculate the time it should take to get to a point. The ETE will help you sail the right speed to meet the time requirements of each leg, but ETE changes with speed and course, so you need an additional timer to keep track of the time elapsed on each leg. It would be nice to have a countdown timer that could be set at the beginning of each leg to keep track of the absolute time you have to get to the next waypoint. As long as the time on the countdown timer matches the ETE, everything will be all right. The only alternative to a countdown timer is to subtract the elapsed time from the time allowed for each leg, but doing the math is inconvenient especially when a timer countdown will do it for you. The receiver does not have one, but your watch does, so you plan to use it.

On the day of the race, you have the chart, the tables you made and your receiver. A boat leaves every 10 minutes and your turn finally arrives. You turn the receiver on and activate the route. The steering page shows the bearing to P1A as 186°, so you shove off and keep an eye on the compass until you reach that heading. According to plan, it should take 23 minutes to reach P1A, so you set the countdown timer and activate it. You tell the crew to put on sails until you reach the desired speed of 8.3 knots. You immediately notice that the ETE is not stable. It does not count down at one second intervals, but jumps down a few seconds, then up even more. Sometimes it suddenly changes by up to a minute. This type of behavior occurs only when your course meanders or your speed fluctuates. You check your compass and grip the helm sternly to bring the ship to a steady speed and course. After doing everything you know how, the seconds of the ETE still change unpredictably, but the minute reading seems stable and usable. You decide to rely on only the minute part of the ETE. The countdown timer says you need to be at P1A in 19:30 while the ETE is around 20 minutes, which is pretty close, but you still decide to compensate for your slightly slow start by putting on a bit more speed. When your speed reaches 8.9 knots, the ETE drops to about 16 minutes while the countdown timer is 17:31. It looks like a game of cat and mouse between the timers.

"Ship ahead!" one of the crew calls from the bow. You blast your horn because sailboats have right-of-way, but the other ship does not move. You blast again, but there is no response, so you take evasive maneuvers. As you steer your boat hard to the left, the arrow on the compass navigation screen points far to the right showing the direction you need to turn to get back on course. You switch to the map screen to see that you are headed away from the direct line course to P1 and P1A.

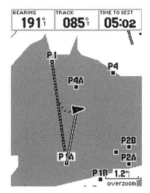

Once past the obstacle, you turn once more toward P1A, but the bearing to get there has changed from 186° to 193°. You bring the boat around and try to get as close to the correct bearing as possible.

The countdown reports 9:30 to arrive, but the ETE is bouncing around 15 minutes. You put on more sails and at 12 knots the two timers almost match. It is straight sailing until the receiver signals the change in direction to get to P1B. You make a quick note of the time it took to get to P1A and with an eye on the compass, you bring the boat around to 129°. You made it to P1A in 22:47, so you reduce your speed from 12 knots to the 9 the plan allows to get to P1B. You also set the countdown timer to 8 minutes and start it.

"Cable ship ahead!" you hear from above. You are in a cable area, but you did not know they would be working the weekend. They certainly will not move, so you had better do so. You veer hard to the right to get around then return to course. The countdown timer says 4:18, but the ETE is somewhere close to 6 minutes. More speed, but there is another obstacle. A group of fishing boats are bringing in their nets, so you steer around them too. Once clear you have 2:08 to get to P1B, but the ETE at your present speed is over 5 minutes. You take a look at the moving map. What a mess!

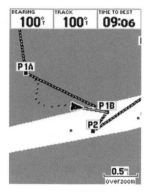

It took 10:15 to get to P1B, which means you have to subtract the 2:12 you went over from the time it takes to get from P1B to P2, so you have 2:48 left. You set the countdown timer and bring the ship around to 229° to head for P2. It is a short distance and fortunately the way looks clear. You find that 10 knots is too fast, so you slow down until the ETE is close to the countdown timer. When you arrive, you are ahead of schedule by 30 seconds, but after you snap the photo of the race marker and get started again, you note it took 2:31 seconds for the leg. The adjusted time was 2:48, so things are looking good.

The next leg should take 11 minutes. You reset your timer and assume a heading of 69° as you try to get up to the target speed of 7.1 knots as fast as possible.

It is smooth sailing to get to P2A until you get close and can see there is more cable work going on in the area of P2B, so you decide to make a change in the route. Instead of going around the small island closer to P2B, you will sail between it and the main island. The time to go from P2A to P2B and P2B to P3 is 10 minutes. As you are now going directly from P2A to P3, you have 10 minutes to do it. It is not a straight

A watch with a countdown timer complements the ETE time.

path to P3, so you will set the timer and use the ETE as a guide, not as an exact measure. You will use the tactic of covering most the distance quickly and slowing down a lot once you are headed directly to P3 and the ETE can be compared against the countdown timer. You will ignore the bearing the receiver gives until you can go directly toward P3.

When you arrive at P2A, you start the timer, but you do not do anything to the receiver. Many receivers can figure out when you head to a non-adjacent point in a route that it too should skip and direct you to the next closest waypoint. You cover most of the distance at about 7 knots, so when you come close to P3 you have about 2 minutes to go. By now the receiver is pointing to P3 and you slow your speed so the ETE almost matches the countdown timer. A quick look at the moving map shows the detour you took.

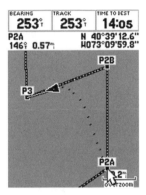

Your plan worked out great because you reached P3 in 10:22. You take the photo, set the timer, change your heading to 11° and try to pick up speed as fast as possible to reach your target of 11.6 knots. The total elapsed time from P1 to P3 is 56:50 while the allotted time is 57 minutes, so you are doing great!

The trip to P4 was not exactly straight because you had to get around a few obstacles, but the receiver's ETE calculation and the countdown timer keep you on schedule and you arrive a little under at 12:25. You and the crew are working like a finely tuned machine, at least until you try to take the picture. In an effort to get as close as possible, you lean over the side of the boat. You snap the photo, but when you try to get back your feet slip and you let go of the camera. You and the rest of the crew watch as it sinks to the dismal depths. You know the race is over—at least for your crew. Losing the camera means disqualification. Your time will not even be recorded.

You all decide to sail on as though nothing happened. Back at the helm you man the timer and receiver. It takes 11:48 to get to P4A and finally 13:18 to reach the finish line. Your total time is 94:21, which looks pretty good when compared against the 94 minutes set for the course. It is the closest you have ever come and if only you had not dropped the camera the first prize might have been yours.

10 Using a Computer and Topographical Maps

The previous chapters illustrated how to take coordinates from a map, program them into a receiver and use them on a trip. A computer can remove the drudgery of measuring coordinates from a map and typing them into a receiver. The various ways in which a computer can be used in conjunction with a GPS receiver are explored in Chapter 13: GPS Receivers and Personal Computers; however, this chapter illustrates how computer based maps can be used to plan a hiking trip.

You have had a computer and a GPS receiver for several years, but you have never connected your receiver to your computer. Your situation changed when you bought Terrain Navigator Pro produced by Maptech®. You selected Terrain Navigator Pro over the less expensive Terrain Navigator because the Pro version includes recent aerial photographs in addition to the USGS topographical maps. Aerial photos enable you to look at recent photos of the same area covered by the map, so you can see any man-made features that have changed since the map was last updated. You will use the software not only to plan trips and transfer the waypoints and routes to the receiver, but you will also use it to record and display any waypoints you mark in the field.

You have visited Chiricahua National Monument in southeastern Arizona several times over the years. You find the strange landscape fascinating. You have a trip planned for the area and this time you will climb to the top of Chiricahua Peak, spend the night there, then descend the next day. You immediately install your new software and search for the word "Chiricahua".

The Place Finder routine in the program searches the maps and finds all the places that have the word Chiricahua in them. You are amazed to see a place called Chiricahua Natural Bridge. You have been to the park many times and never heard about it. You double click on the name and the map instantly appears showing the location of the natural bridge.

The Place Finder panel reports back ten locations with Chiricahua in their name.

The map shows the natural bridge to be close to the Monument Headquarters, so you select the marker tool and place a marker at the location of the bridge on the map. You access the edit marker menu to change the waypoint name from the automatically generated name to "Nat Bridge". The coordinate of the waypoint is also shown. Get-

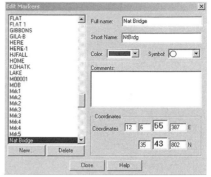

Renaming the waypoint marker. Its coordinate is also shown.

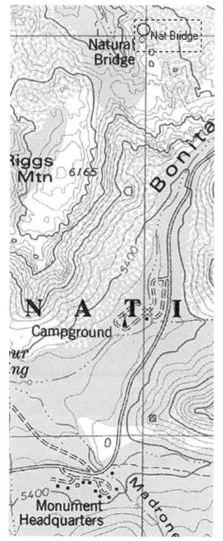

Monument headquarters at the bottom, Natural Bridge at the top.

ting the coordinate of the natural bridge was as easy as clicking the computer mouse. You did not have to use a ruler or eyeball it. It was so easy to get the coordinate; you wonder why you waited so long to get map software.

You have never been to the natural bridge even though it is close to the monument entrance. The contour lines between the road and the bridge show that the elevation changes from approximately 5400 ft. to about 5960 ft., but they are close together, so there is the possibility of cliffs or a very steep hike. You switch to the three-dimensional (3D) mode to visualize the change in elevation. The 3D view shows a cliff between the bridge and the road. Rotating the 3D view shows that the bridge is isolated and difficult to get to. The map does not show any trails leading to the bridge from any direction. You put it on your list of places to explore.

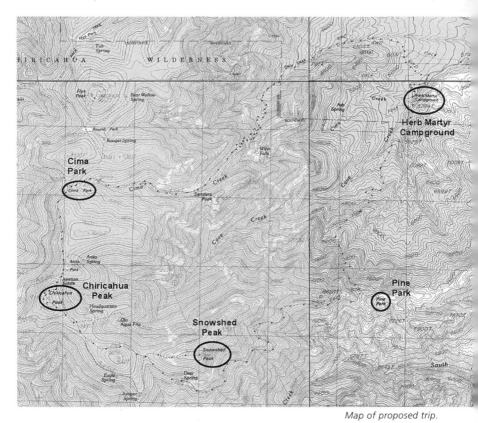

Map of proposed trip.

You return to the Place Finder screen and double click on Chiricahua Peak. Instantly, the peak appears on your computer screen. You zoom out and search for possible trails leading from the valley floor to the peak. Rather quickly, you determine the best path is to leave from the Herb Martyr campground, hike an established trail to Cima Park then on to Chiricahua Peak. There you will

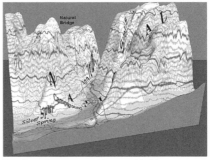

3D view of area around natural bridge.

spend the night and return the next day by way of Snowshed Peak and past Pine Park. The route looks feasible and the plan reasonable, but the mapping program provides tools to give you invaluable information. You switch to the 3D mode.

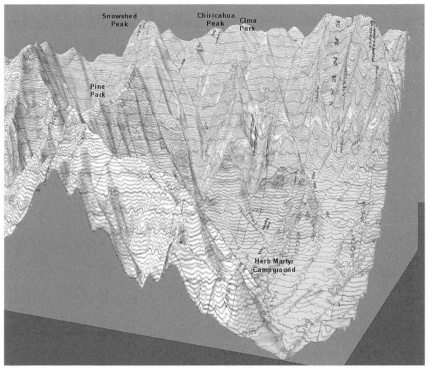

3D view of proposed trip.

The first thing you notice in the 3D view is the big vertical ascent. You are a good hiker, but you want to have a nice enjoyable hike, not a death march. You switch back to the 2D map mode and activate the distance tool. Using the distance tool, you trace

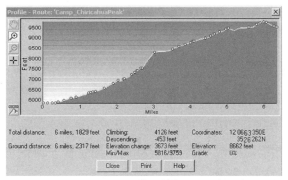

Profile of hike up to Chiricahua Peak.

your proposed route from the campground to the summit. When you are done, you select the line you traced and activate the profile tool.

The profile shows the distance from the campground to the camping place southeast of the peak to be just over 6 mi (9.7 km). The vertical change, however, is nearly 4300 ft. (1310.6 m). For you, that much change in elevation in a single day is a hard hike. You search the map for a nice camping spot halfway to the summit. No place is suitable. The best camping areas are all around 9000 ft. (2743.2 m), which is almost as high as the peak. You decide to modify your plan to start the hike earlier in the day and to stay an extra day on the peak to rest, explore and enjoy yourself to make up for all the hard work getting there.

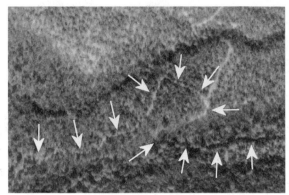

Portion of the trail visible from the aerial photos are indicated by arrows.

You choose your route along a trail shown on the map. You know that the USGS topographical maps have not updated trails or man-made structures for at least a couple of decades, so it is possible that the trail no longer exists. That is where spending the extra money to access aerial photos is advantageous. You zoom into the area you will be hiking and switch to the aerial photo mode. The aerial photos are automatically loaded. You search along the trail you marked and from the photos you can see the road to the campground has changed and you can also distinctly see some of the trail at the start of your proposed route. Where you can see the trail, it looks really good. The trail is most visible where it cuts through vegetation. Enough of the trail is visible that you believe your hiking plan is feasible, but you know, even before arriving, that the return trail may be hard to find, so you check the waypoints for the last part of the trail. The number and proximity of the waypoints for

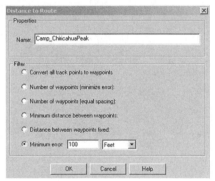

Converting a distance line to a route.

New Route Information	
Name:	Camp_ChiricahuaPeak
Waypoints:	56
Error:	98 feet
Average Spacing:	627 feet
Shortest Leg:	156 feet
Longest Leg:	2937 feet

OK

Route conversion results.

the last part of the hike look adequate, so you feel prepared. Technology is so powerful. You wonder when you will be able to look at live satellite images of a planned hiking area from your desk.

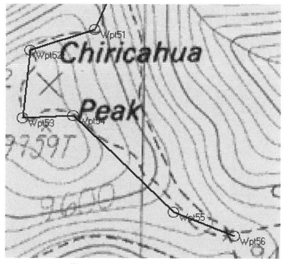

The route corresponds closely to the marked trail.

Your proposed route looks good, so you want to change it into a route you can use in your GPS receiver. You select the tool to convert a distance line into a route with waypoints. After you type in the route name, you are offered several options. You select the option where the route generated is within 100 ft. (30.5 m) of the drawn line. An information box pops up to report the results of the conversion. The greatest deviation from the drawn line is 98 ft. (29.9 m) and there are 56 waypoints in the route.

You wonder how close the route really is to the line you drew over the marked trail. You zoom in to see that the route corresponds closely to the trail. You

Waypoints in the route to Chiricahua Peak.

activate the route waypoint list and select "Wpt3." The waypoint coordinate is measure to the meter and it did not require a ruler or any typing on either a computer or a receiver. You finish your planning by tracing the return route from the peak; you look at its profile then convert it to a route.

Before you go any further, you print a copy of the map and the intended route, so you can have it with you on the trail. While you are printing, you notice the heavy lines on the map. You know that the thinner lines are UTM grid lines, but you do not know what the heavier lines mean. You select the information cursor and select the lines. You learn that the heavy lines represent the boundaries of the

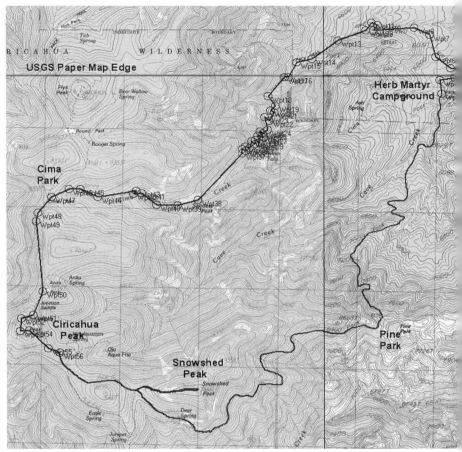

Planned routes to and from Chiricahua Peak.

USGS 1:24,000 paper maps. The computer program abuts the maps, so they seamlessly cover the entire state. Your route uses four USGS maps:

Chiricahua Peak
Rustler Park
Portal
Portal Peak

You are about done planning your trip. The planning went faster than it ever has before and you know more about the trail and the character of the hike with a lot less effort. You need to transfer the waypoints to your receiver for use on the hike, so you activate the screen that allows you to select the receiver type. You select your receiver and the serial port on your computer to which the receiver is connected.

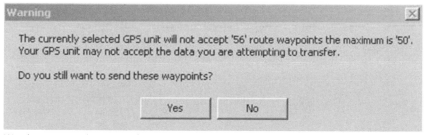

Warning message during transfer to receiver.

You start the transfer and every-thing seems to be going fine until a warning message appears on your computer screen. On no! When you formed the route, you told the program to use as many waypoints as it took to keep the error below 100 ft. (30.5 m). The program pro-duced 56 waypoints and your re-ceiver has a limit of 50 waypoints per route. You should have se-lected the second or third conver-sion option (Number of waypoints) and specified a maximum of 50 waypoints. You do not want the route of 56 waypoints transferred to the receiver because the receiver will delete the last waypoints from the route in order to make it fit. You select "no" then go back to the route on the map. You go to an area of the route where there are a lot of switchbacks and the way-points are close together. You can probably live with less accuracy in the switchbacks, so you delete enough points to have only 50 waypoints in the route. You acti-vate the transfer again and every-thing works.

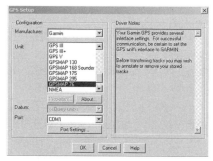

Setting up to transfer information to the receiver.

Sending a route from the computer to the receiver.

On the receiver you to go the route list and look at the route you just transferred. A scan of the waypoints shows that they are all there and the total length of the route as shown on the receiver is just over 6 mi (9.7 km). You transfer the return route to the receiver and it too looks correct. When you display the entire trip on the receiver's screen, it looks just like it should. You look at one of the waypoints on the route to the peak. The coordinate checks out when you eyeball its position on the map. It took hardly any work on your part to get two routes full of accurate coordinates into your receiver. If you were not emotionally attached to your old paper maps, they would end up in the garbage tomorrow.

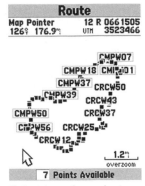

Entire trip on the receiver's screen.

The day of the trip arrives. Early in the morning, you fire up your receiver and start up the hill. It is every bit as hard a climb as you thought it would be, but the views at the top and camping for two days in total peace make it worth the effort. While you explore the area around the peak, you mark several waypoints. You know you will be able to transfer them from your receiver to the map program when you get home. You have stopped wondering why you did not buy the computer map program before and are just glad you did.

A waypoint from the route generated on the computer.

11 Recovering from Disaster

In all the previous examples, the GPS receiver performed flawlessly. It provided sure knowledge of your current position and guided you, with the Goto and Route functions, to where you wanted to go. The results described in the previous chapters are completely achievable, but you still need to be prepared to cope with poor signal reception and possibly the entire loss of the receiver. This chapter stresses manual navigation techniques. Refer also to the books listed on page 205 if you would like to be more proficient with a map and compass. Read also Chapter 3, which describes the importance of field notes to track your path.

The Lava Flows

Your neighbor owns a cabin in Duck Creek Village, and at the yearly block party he tells you about the lava flows in the middle of the forest. It does not seem too interesting until he tells you that there are supposed to be huge underground tunnels that stretch for hundreds of miles. He has not seen them himself, but claims the locals know all about them. You had read about a lava tube, in an excellent Arizona guidebook, that is like a railway tunnel snaking under the forest floor. It sounded fascinating, so you decided to look for the tunnels near Duck Creek. You buy the USGS Henrie Knolls map of southern Utah.

Your neighbor said there were openings near Anderson Spring and near the two peaks east-southeast of the spring. As you can only spare one weekend, you and a friend will drive to Duck Creek on Friday after work, search for the tubes on Saturday, fish in the lake on Sunday, then return home.

You have owned a GPS receiver for quite a while. It has always worked and you have come to rely on it. You generally use a map, but take a compass only out of habit. You will take the trip in late September when the cooler weather has killed all the mosquitoes. The receiver calculates the sunrise and sunset to be 6:17 am and 6:30 pm respectively. You will leave from Duck Lake and hike up a dry creekbed to the point labeled #1. The receiver's map screen will be used to guide you over the large lava flow to the two small hills labeled TWOPKS. From there it will be on to Anderson Spring. The return trip will be across the lava flow to the south to a point labeled #2, then back to #1 and down the creekbed. The total trip is about 7.5 mi. (12.1 km). It is light for only 12 hours, which is not a long day, but if you leave camp at 6:00 am there will be enough time to make the trip and do some exploring.

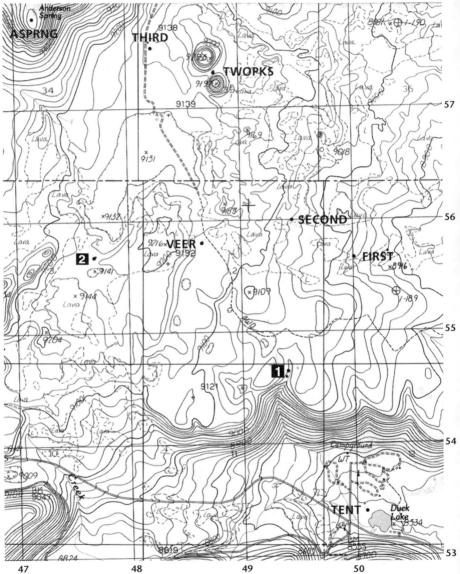

USGS Henrie Knolls, Utah (1:24,000 scale).

The Trip

The Friday for the trip finally arrives. The second work ends, you rush to pick up your friend and you're off. It is dark by the time you arrive at Duck Lake, but because it is late in the camping season there are only a few other campers and it is easy to find a deluxe spot for your tent right on the shore.

In the morning, you are up before sunrise and right at 5:45 you turn the receiver on to mark the camp's position:

12 S   350207m.E.   4153453m.N.   TENT

You jot the coordinate down in your notebook along with the time. The mouth of the dry creek is not as easy to find as you thought it would be and it is not until 7:00 am that the ground levels off at what should be the end of the creek. You pull out your receiver just to verify your position, but after five minutes it still has not locked onto the satellite signals. The satellite status screen shows there are six satellites in the area, but only two have strong signals. You know foliage will block the signals, so you walk around trying to see if they get stronger at different positions. Nothing seems to work, which is strange because you have hiked and biked all over and your receiver has always been able to pick up enough satellites to lock on to. The growth in this forest does not seem more dense than any of the others where the receiver worked flawlessly. You wish you had brought your remote antenna because its higher performance and increased sensitivity would help in a situation like this. You look at the map and find a four-wheel drive road due north. Maybe it will provide enough of an opening to allow the receiver to lock, so you head north. You make a note that it is 7:10 am.

As you walk, you notice the beauty of the forest. The sunlight filters through the trees, a slight breeze stirs the quaking aspens and birds sing as they flutter and chase each other. Forty minutes later, you still have not found the road. The map must be out-of-date, but it does not pose a problem because soon you will reach a lava flow where it will certainly be clear enough for the receiver to lock. Sure enough, at 8:10 am you step out of the forest onto a rough and broken lava flow. When you reach the edge of the flow, your receiver locks and you store your position as FIRST.

12 S   350018m.E.   4155622m.N.   FIRST

When you look at the map, you discover you are way off course. The plan was to go directly from the creekbed to TWOPKS shown at the top of the map. You could kick yourself for not using your compass because you now have a lot of extra walking ahead of you.

The map shows you need to cross through a stretch of forest before you hit the flow that leads to TWOPKS. The receiver will work on the flow, but not in the thick forest, so from now on you will use your compass to stay on course when the receiver cannot lock. You enter the coordinate for TWOPKS into the receiver:

12 S   348700m.E.   4157400m.N.   TWOPKS

You set the receiver to report magnetic coordinates, then use the point-to-point calculation to determine that the bearing between FIRST and TWOPKS is 303°. Once you enter the forest and try to sight a bearing, you discover how dense it really is because you can only sight a short distance ahead. Walking the bearing with absolute precision is not vital because as soon as you get onto the next flow the receiver will determine your position, but staying on course will save time. Using your compass and a bit of care, you work your way to the next lava flow.

It is 9:10 am before you are far enough out on the second flow to get a lock with the receiver. You mark the position as SECOND.

12 S   349567m.E.   4156021m.N.   SECOND

Just to see how well you stayed on course, you have the receiver calculate the bearing from FIRST to SECOND. When the receiver reports the bearing as 278°, you know you were not very careful because you were off by 25°. The receiver works fine as long as you are on the flow and you use it to continue your journey. After almost two hours of climbing over the lava boulders that litter the uneven flow, you arrive at TWOPKS where you search until noon for lava tubes, with no luck. After lunch, you head in a general westerly direction until you reach another flow where the receiver locks and you mark your position as THIRD.

12 S   348257m.E.   4157602m.N.   THIRD

You will have to use your compass to get through the forest to Anderson Spring and you want the receiver to tell you the bearing, so you enter Anderson Spring's coordinate into the receiver:

12 S   347200m.E.   4157800m.N.   ASPRNG

The bearing between the two points is reported as 272°. Exercising more care, you use your compass to walk the bearing and arrive at the spring at 1:15 pm. During the hike to the spring, you have written times, positions and bearings in your notebook as follows:

- 5:45 am   TENT: 350207 4153453
                  Nobody else up. Very quiet.
- 7:10 am   Receiver no lock. North to 4WD road.
- 8:35 am   FIRST: 350018 4155622
                  TWOPKS: 348700 4157400
                  FIRST to TWOPKS 303°.
- 9:10 am   SECOND: 349567 4156021
                  FIRST to SECOND 278°.
- 10:58 am   Arrive at TWOPKS.
- 12:00 pm   Lunch. No tubes at TWOPKS.
- 12:20 pm   Start for Anderson.
- 12:36 pm   THIRD: 348257 4157602
                  Close to road.
                  ASPRNG: 347200 4157800
                  THIRD to ASPRNG 272°.
- 1:15 pm   Arrive at Anderson Spring.

You use the information and estimate that it will take about 3.5 hours to get back to camp. You do not want to get caught by darkness, which means you have until 3:00 pm to search for tubes. When the time to return arrives, you have not found anything that even remotely resembles a lava tube. Disappointed, you prepare for the trip back by entering the coordinate for point #2 and calculate a bearing of 152° to get there. Using the compass, you start back.

The Disaster

Only 15 minutes later, you slip while climbing over a huge log. Fortunately, your fall is broken. Unfortunately, your fall is broken by your receiver. It is dented and you know it is inoperable because nothing appears on the screen when you turn it on. Slight panic sets in. You depended on the receiver to give you precise knowledge of your position. Navigating with map and compass alone is nothing new, but GPS technology has changed your mode of navigation. You no longer confine your movements to take you from one recognizable landform to the next. You just hike without much thought of where you are and occasionally use the receiver to find your position.

Your first concern is getting back to camp before dark. You do have a flashlight, but no extra batteries. You could survive a night outside, but it does get rather cold and you prefer to sleep in your tent. You open your notebook to study the times and locations you recorded. Dead reckoning tells you that you are about 0.25 mi. (0.4 km) south of Anderson Spring. It dawns on you that the confidence the receiver provided is gone. You are back to the days of "I think we're about here." Your notebook convinces you that crossing the lava flows is much slower than going through the forest. It also reminds you of the road you saw near THIRD. It will be a lot faster to go directly to the road and take it south. You hope it goes as far as the map shows, as the four-wheel drive road is also shown, and it no longer exists. You will just have to take it as far as it goes.

Your new plan quickly jells. Head due east until you hit the road. Follow the road until it either ends or turns into a trail. It should end by a flow. From the end of the road, walk a bearing of 160° for 0.25 mi. (0.4 km), to get clear of any lava flows. From that point you will veer to a bearing of 134° until you run into the camp, the lake or the highway. Then you will return to your tent.

Due east is 90° on the map, but you need to account for the east 14° declination. You repeat the phrase "East is least, West is best" to remind yourself that true north bearings are converted to magnetic bearings by subtracting east or adding west declinations. You subtract 14° from 90°, dial in 76° into your compass and start moving. Much to your relief, at 4:45 pm you arrive at the road. You are not quite sure where you are, but at 5:50 pm the road ends. There is one more hour of daylight with just over 2 mi. (3.2 km) to go. You count paces until you have gone approximately 0.25 mi. (0.4 km) from the end of the road on a bearing of 160°. You think you are around the point labeled VEER on the map. You set the compass for 134° and carefully walk the bearing.

The sun sets while you are still walking, but you have started a sharp descent. Within minutes, you see the light of a fire. Someone is just ahead. When the people around the campfire tell you that you are in the Duck Lake campground, you suppress a small leap of joy. You will soon be back at your tent to spend a warm night. The batteries in your flashlight go dead before you can find your tent. It is like amnesia has struck. You cannot find your tent and you cannot seem to remember where you saw it last. You ask a passing Forest Ranger for help. "Oh, we confiscated the tent this morning. You should have read the signs: no camping on the shore."

12 GPS on the Road

GPS receivers for use in automobiles are the most advanced receivers on the market. They combine electronic maps, automatic route generation and GPS position calculations. GPS receivers designed for cars are significantly more expensive than the handheld receivers presented in earlier chapters, so it is helpful to understand what they can do that less expensive receivers cannot.

The most important capabilities that distinguish automotive GPS receivers from other receivers are:

- Automatic route generation (autoroute)
- Turn-by-turn instructions

Autorouting means that the receiver is capable of plotting a course from one point to a destination, along roads and highways, without any input from the user. Autorouting is different from routes formed using downloadable maps or routes formed by sequential waypoints.

A receiver capable of accepting downloadable maps, but incapable of automatically calculating a route, will display the map, but it will not display a route that follows the roads. Assume you download some street maps into your GPS receiver. Assume also that you use the computer to calculate a route between two points. The route calculated by the computer and displayed on the computer will follow the roads and highways. The route it calculates will detail each place where a turn must be made, but the road on the map between turns acts as the route. If you transfer a route that follows the roads on a computer to a receiver that does not have autorouting capability, the direction of travel between turns will not follow the road, but will be shown as a straight line. See the GPS screenshot on the next page. The solid, black triangle represents your car. The line indicated by the light colored arrow is the route between your current position and where you need to go. It is impossible to drive the straight route shown because it does not follow the roads. If a receiver is incapable of calculating routes, it can only indicate the straight-line path between any two points. Although the route was correctly calculated and displayed on the computer when it was transferred to the receiver, it became meaningless because the receiver is incapable of making the route follow the roads.

Route Properties

| Name: | 1710LNGDLD to CHRCHLDWNS | | | ☑ Autoname | | OK |

Waypoints (2): ☐ Center map on selected item

Directions/Name	Distance	Leg Length	Leg Time	Course
1710LNGDLD	0 ft			
Get on Longdale Dr and drive west	0 ft	0 ft	00:00:00	238° true
Turn left onto N Military Hwy	0.212 mi	0.211 mi	00:00:23	244° true
Turn right onto Norview Ave	0.734 mi	0.523 mi	00:01:17	150° true
Exit right onto ramp onto I-64	1.07 mi	0.333 mi	00:00:39	239° true
Keep right onto I-64	4.05 mi	2.98 mi	00:03:10	310° true
Keep left onto I-64	16.3 mi	12.2 mi	00:11:21	285° true
Take exit 79 to the right onto I-64	93.7 mi	77.4 mi	01:11:11	319° true
Take exit 94 to the right onto US 340	186.1 mi	92.4 mi	01:25:11	278° true
Turn left onto US 340	186.3 mi	0.195 mi	00:00:29	316° true
Turn left onto US 11	198.6 mi	12.3 mi	00:12:27	262° true
Exit right onto ramp onto I-64	220.9 mi	22.3 mi	00:21:16	226° true
Take exit 101 to the left onto I-64	402.1 mi	181.2 mi	02:46:49	359° true
Continue towards I64 West/Frankfort/Louisville	577.5 mi	175.3 mi	02:40:56	310° true
Take exit 124-B to the right onto I 264 East/I 264 West/Watter	639.6 mi	62.1 mi	00:57:06	279° true
Keep left onto I-264 ramp	639.8 mi	0.231 mi	00:00:34	319° true
Take exit 10 to the right onto 3rd Street/Ky 1020/Southern Pkwy	649.0 mi	9.12 mi	00:09:24	248° true
Turn right onto Southern Pkwy	649.0 mi	390 ft	00:00:11	289° true
Turn left onto Oakdale Ave	649.8 mi	0.738 mi	00:01:03	7° true
Turn left onto Central Ave	650.1 mi	0.322 mi	00:00:35	8° true
CHRCHLDWNS	650.4 mi	0.268 mi	00:01:03	187° true

Buttons: Cancel, Insert..., Find..., Edit, Delete, Recalculate, Invert, Show On Map

Total Distance: 650.4 mi, Total Time: 10:05:05

Each turn required in the route is described. © Garmin. Reproduced with permission.

The figure below left shows the results of autorouting. The triangle represents our position and the dark-colored arrow touches the route. Note that the route follows the roads. The actual points in the route, as mentioned above, are the places where turns must be made. The computer screenshot above shows an automatically generated route between 1710 Longdale Drive, Virginia and Churchill Downs, Kentucky. Not only is every required turn in the list, but also a description of how the turn is to be made. Explicit turn-by-turn instructions make it possible to make the trip without looking at the GPS receiver display; however, the map on the receiver display allows you to see the big picture.

Autorouting is required to make routes conform to the roads on the map.

Autorouting calculates and displays routes that follow the roads. © Garmin.

	Turn left on N Military Hwy	269°	02:46ᴬ
	Turn right on Norview Ave	0.6ᵐ	02:48ᴬ
	Exit right to I-64(N)	0.9ᵐ	02:48ᴬ
	Arrive at Churchill Downs Inc	654ᵐ	12:52ᴬ

Turn-by-turn instructions are displayed on the receiver screen. © Garmin.

Most receivers allow the user to specify priorities used by the receiver to calculate the route. Each time the receiver must make a trade off it looks at the priorities set by the user. The user can specify:

Route calculation for:
Faster time
Shorter distance
Direct route

Route should avoid:
Highways
Toll roads
U-Turns
Specific streets, highways or roads

Another aspect of autorouting is how the receiver responds when you stray off the planned course. If you run into road construction or a closed road and have to go off the previously planned course, a receiver capable of autorouting can determine a new route from your current position to the destination. Automatic recalculation of the route when you stray allows you to take a road that you know is better than the calculated route, yet depend on the receiver when you are in unfamiliar territory. Autorouting enables the receiver to automatically update the route regardless of how far astray you went.

Automatic recalculation of the route also helps to cope with map inaccuracies. No map, regardless of whether it is paper or electronic, is completely accurate. Roads are always changing and it is next to impossible to ensure that a map is completely up-to-date. Not only can new roads not appear on a map, but also at times, proposed roads yet to be built, find their way on to a map. Regardless of the cause of the error, the situation will occur when the map on the receiver screen tells

Navman iCN-630 receiver.

you one thing, yet the road in front of your eyes tells you something else. In such a situation, you obviously follow what you see and let the receiver recalculate the route based on the maneuvers you make.

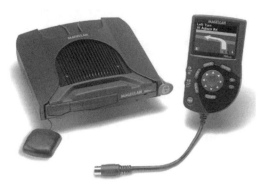

Calculating a route requires a lot of processing power, so before you buy a receiver see if you can test it out or talk to your friends to see if calculating routes is

Magellan 750 Nav+ receiver for automobiles.

done in a reasonable amount of time. The acid test of route-calculating speed is when you leave a pre-planned route and the receiver is forced to calculate a new route from your current location to the destination. If the receiver takes too long calculating the route, you could miss a critical turn and be stuck on a freeway, headed the wrong direction, before the receiver finishes. Obsolete or old map data also forces the receiver to recalculate. If the road of the pre-planned route no longer exists, you cannot travel it and you will have to go off route, thereby forcing the receiver to calculate a new route. Fast route calculation is critical.

Memory is also important. The maps used by the GPS receiver either have to be downloaded into the receiver's built-in memory, or onto a memory stick. Most receivers in this class accept memory sticks, which are programmed over a USB link to your PC; however, the Magellan 750 Nav+ has a hard drive in it that holds all of the maps, so there is not need to ever transfer maps from your computer to the receiver. The more memory available for maps, the more territory you can cover using highly detailed maps.

All receivers of this class have a base map, so even if you don't have a more detailed downloadable map you can always navigate to an area. Without the downloadable map you are missing more than just road information. Detailed maps include point-of-interest locations like hotels, rest areas, restaurants, shopping, entertainment, emergency services, amusement parks, museums and other tourist attractions.

In order to have access to all the maps you may need you have a number of choices. Purchase enough memory sticks to carry all the maps with you; go on short trips where all the data fits into a single stick; take your laptop PC along to transfer maps as needed; or purchase a system that contains all the maps without requiring any transfers.

Garmin Street Pilot III.

Another thing to consider is the antenna. Some GPS receivers designed for vehicles come with external antennas for placement on the roof of the car. If the receiver you choose does not include an external antenna, purchase one. The screens on the automobile receivers are larger than most handheld receiver screens, but you may at times want to take a closer look. If you have an external antenna, you can take the receiver from off the dash and either look at it more closely yourself or pass it to another person in the car even if they are in the back seat. The cost of the external antenna may seem like a lot, but the flexibility and convenience it allows when using the receiver is worth the money.

Most receivers marketed for the automobile can also talk to the user to provide audible driving instructions. Voice instructions are very convenient because they free you from looking at the screen each time there is a change in directions. If you are driving alone, voice instructions can make your drive safer.

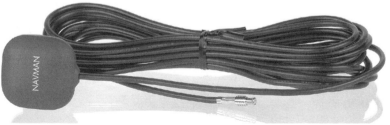

External antenna for the Navman iCN-630.

Use is Simple

Using a GPS receiver designed for an automobile is simple. First, if the receiver does not already have all the maps required, download them into the receiver or the memory stick. The next step depends on whether you are already in the car or if you are planning a trip in advance. If you are already in the car and the receiver is locked onto the satellites, select where you want to go, tell the receiver to create a route and it will lead you there. It is as easy as that. If you are planning a trip in advance and wish to store it in the receiver's memory for later use, you need to select a starting point. The receiver will plan the route from the starting point to the destination, you can store it in memory and when the day comes to make the trip, you simply activate the route.

Selecting where to go is easy. As mentioned above, the electronic maps have not only road information, but also points-of-interest. Finding a hotel or restaurant is simple because the receiver allows you to search for points-of-interest much like you search for waypoints on a handheld receiver. You can either search for a specific type of place by proximity, which means the closest one to your current location, or by name. Have you ever been on a long trip and wondered where the closest service station, restaurant or hotel is? The receiver can now tell you the answer and that is not all—it can take you there. Destinations can also be found by searching by address or even by intersection.

Searching for the nearest points-of-interest.

The points-of-interest are not all inclusive. If the map database does not contain a specific location, it cannot lead you to it. Certainly, you could find the location independently and mark it as a waypoint, but if you had to do that for every place you wanted to visit, it would defeat the convenience and power of having such a receiver. So, if you have a favorite hotel or restaurant chain, you may want to ask, before you buy, if your favorite locations are part of the database.

Searching for points-of-interest alphabetically by name.

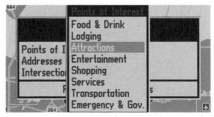

Selecting a type location from list of points-of-interest.

13 GPS Receivers and Personal Computers

If your current use of a receiver does not involve a computer, it should. The most important feature of a computer program designed to work with a GPS receiver is the program's ability to transfer data to and from the receiver. The type of information transferred between the computer and the receiver depends on the type of program you buy and the capabilities of the receiver. There are three classes of programs available for use with a GPS receiver. Their capabilities and what they transfer to and from the receiver are described below.

Non-Map

- Use to manage waypoints
- Enter waypoints on computer, transfer to receiver for use
- Mark waypoints in the field, transfer to the computer for storage
- Inexpensive, shareware programs suitable
- Transfers waypoints, routes and track log

Computer Based Maps

- Map database is the most important part of the software
- Provides maps on computer screen (roads or topographical)
- Trip planning tools
- Transfers waypoints (not maps) to receiver for use in field
- Transfers data marked in field to computer for display on map on computer screen
- Available from several vendors
- Transfers waypoints, routes and track log

Downloadable Maps

- Transferability of map to receiver is most important part
- Map displayed on computer then transferred to receiver to display on receiver screen
- Trip planning tools
- Waypoints also transfer to and from receiver
- Also used to manage waypoints

- Available only from receiver manufacturer
- Transfers waypoints, routes, track log and actual map data

Your use of your receiver will determine which class of program will be most useful for you, but at a bare minimum all users will find the non-map programs to be useful and highly affordable.

Using a receiver in conjunction with a computer requires the receiver to be capable of interfacing with the computer. Fortunately, most receivers are. However, be sure that the receiver can connect to a computer before buying it. Most receivers currently connect to the computer's serial port.

Transferring map data can take a long time over a serial port. A receiver capable of using the computer's USB port will be able to transfer data faster. Connecting a receiver to a computer is simple and using the programs is easy. Furthermore, computers extend the storage capability of your receiver and make it more fun to use.

Non-Map Program

If you currently are not using a computer with your GPS receiver or you do not want to spend the money to get a map-based program, you should acquire and learn to use a GPS waypoint management program. Shareware waypoint management programs like GPS Utility, MacGPS and Waypoint+ are affordable. At a bare minimum, they will make entering waypoint coordinates from a paper map much easier than typing them directly into the receiver. All GPS receiver owners should avail themselves of the capability provided by a non-map program.

Non-map waypoint programs are capable of:

- Entering waypoint names, coordinates and comments
- Forming routes
- Viewing waypoint, route and track log data on the screen

Editing or entering a waypoint on the computer. ©GPS Utility Limited. Reproduced with permission.

Editing or displaying a route.
©GPS Utility Limited.
Reproduced with permission.

- Storing waypoint, route and track log information on a computer hard drive
- Transferring waypoint, route and track log information to and from a GPS receiver

Although non-map programs display waypoints, routes and track logs on the computer screen with their positions relative to each other, the background is blank unless the user provides a pre-calibrated map.

List of waypoints displayed in GPS Utility. ©GPS Utility Limited. Reproduced with permission.

Non-map programs are best used to:
- Maintain waypoint, route and track log data.
- The large computer screen and keyboard make it much easier to view, manipulate and enter data associated with waypoints, routes and track logs.
- Long-term storage. Most receivers hold between 500 and 1000 waypoints. A non-map program allows you to store tens of thousands of waypoints. Use the computer to store all your GPS information and transfer the data required to the GPS receiver when it is needed. You can also record data while in the field then transfer it to the computer for long-term storage and reference.
- Maintain receiver independent data. Non-map programs can be used to transfer data to any other type of receiver supported by the program. You can transfer your data to a friend's receiver even if it is from another manufacturer or to a new receiver when you upgrade. If you work in a group, like search and rescue, where several receivers of different types are used, the non-map program can be the medium through which data is transferred from a receiver of one manufacturer to that of another manufacturer.

Computer Based Map Programs

The next step up in the hierarchy of computer GPS programs are programs that provide computer based maps in addition to all the data management capabilities of a non-map program.

The most important criterion when selecting a computer based map program is the quality of the maps. You must first determine the type of map that you need, whether it be street or topographical maps, then you must find a program with maps of sufficient accuracy and with up-to-date data. All computer based map programs provide the means to manipulate and store waypoint, route and track log data, thereby making it unnecessary to use a secondary non-map program to manage your data.

Eventually street atlas and topographical map programs will all merge into a single database, but until that day, topographical map programs are provided by companies like Maptech® (Terrain navigator, Terrain navigator Pro), National Geographic Topo!, and DeLorme (Topo). Available road atlas programs are DeLorme Street Atlas USA and Fugawi.

Computer based map programs also act as map databases and provided the ability to search by name or address. Most computer based map programs offer some, if not all, of the capabilities listed on

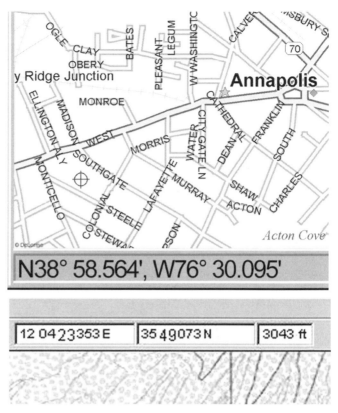

Coordinates at the cursor, the circle with a cross, are automatically displayed.© DeLorme. Reproduced with permission.

N38° 58.564', W76° 30.095'

Topographical map programs provide altitude along with the coordinate. © Maptech. Reproduced with permission.

| 12 0423353 E | 3549073 N | 3043 ft |

pages 167 through 173 in addition to everything offered by a non-map program. Keep in mind, however, that once you have marked way-points or planned a route on the computer that only the waypoints and the routes transfer to the computer. The map information does not transfer. However, there has been a technological development that will allow you to take computer based maps into the field—it is called the Pocket PC. Refer to Chapter 14 to see if the Pocket PC fits into your navigation strategy.

Coordinate Identification

Simply place the cursor on any location and the map program instantly provides its coordinate. Databases of topographical maps also provide the altitude. Virtually all map databases provide coordinates using the latitude/longitude grid system, but some allow the user to select other grids such as UTM or MGRS. It does not really matter which grid is used because you can enter the data into the receiver in one format and then switch to another when necessary and the receiver will make all the conversions.

A lot of time is spent in this book showing how to measure coordinates from a map. An electronic map makes all the manual labor unnecessary. However, do not get rid of your map rulers quite yet or forget everything you learned in the previous chapters, because unless you plan on lugging your portable computer with you on your next hike, you may still need the manual techniques in the field.

A good strategy is to use the computer and the map database program to provide the coordinates of all waypoints that can be identified before the trip and carry a map with an appropriate grid into the field for everything else.

Search Engine

A search engine accepts key words, zip codes, area codes, coordinates, etc., and finds locations or objects that match the specification. The matches are either highlighted or shown on a list. Selecting an object from the match list causes the program to display the object's location on the screen. Search capability is important because map databases are usually very large and cover a lot of area. Instead of panning around the map trying to find a location, simply type in anything you remember about it and let the computer do the rest. If you are trying to find Lake Hiawatha, you would type in Hiawatha and the program would list all potential locations:

Searching a topographical map program for all locations with "knob" in its name. © Maptech. Reproduced with permission.

• Hiawatha Creek
• Hiawatha Falls
• Hiawatha Gulch
• Hiawatha Mountain
• Hiawatha Trail
• Lower Hiawatha Lake
• Mount Hiawatha
• Upper Hiawatha Lake

Searching for 1259 Flamingo Drive in Florida. © Garmin. Reproduced with permission.

The computer did not find Lake Hiawatha, so you have to look at both Upper and Lower Hiawatha Lake to see if they are what you really want.

Searching works on user-specified data also. If you were setting up a cellular telephone network, you would use your GPS receiver to accurately position each transmission tower in the field. Back in the office, you would transfer all the locations to the map using a naming convention to indicate the towers' kilowatt (KW) output as shown below.

Searching for 150 Elm in Castle Rock, Colorado. © Garmin. Reproduced with permission.

    1 KW Towers: T0001_1, T0002_1, T0003_1
    2 KW Towers: T0001_2, T0002_2, T0003_2, T0004_2
    5 KW Towers: T0001_5, T0002_5

The search engine can easily distinguish between the different types of towers, making it easy to instantly locate towers of a given power output on the map.

Marking Locations

Marking a location is another easy way to find a specific place in the future. You can mark and label campsites, river rapids, bird sighting areas, telephone poles, old growth timber stands or anything else. Displaying a marked location on the screen is as simple as choosing its name from a list with the mouse.

Marking the location of Himstant well. © Maptech. Reproduced with permission.

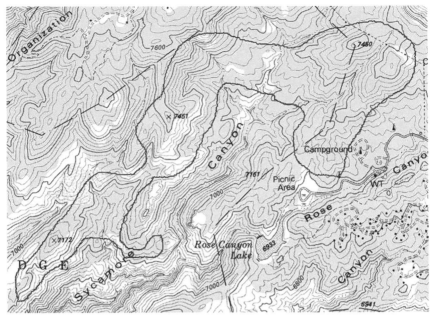

Routes are easily marked for future use. © Maptech. Reproduced with permission.

Marking Routes

Much like a route on a GPS receiver, lists of successive locations can be organized in the map database to show the start, end and all the important points in between. The routes, as formed on the computer, can be transferred to the receiver that guides you in the field. Most programs will provide distance and bearing between each point and total distance just like a GPS receiver.

The power of the computer makes it possible to store hundreds of routes. When combined with a GPS receiver, the computer overcomes the receiver's limited memory and annotation capabilities. The map database program can become the route management tool for personal and business use. You can store the routes of every hike you have ever made on the computer to maintain a lifetime record and to be able to return to any location whenever you like. A uniform laundry business could store its pick-up routes on the database and transfer them to the GPS receiver in the vehicles of new, replacement or temporary drivers.

Distance, Bearing and Area Calculations

Calculating the distance and bearing between two points is easy with a GPS receiver, and of course mapping programs can do much more. A map program can find the length of any path no matter how much it twists or turns. You can draw the path you intend on taking and find the distance before you leave, or you can record waypoints in the field, then transfer them to the computer afterwards to find out how far you went.

Area calculation is a powerful tool that may not be used by most outdoor enthusiasts, but it can be invaluable to professionals. The size of a forest fire can easily be calculated even when fighting the blaze if coordinates from a few of its edges are reported to the central command. The points can be connected using the database program and the area immediately quantified. The size of oil spills, water coverage, mountain acreage

Distance Information		
Start	12 05 27 698E	35 83 659N
Start elevation:	7036 feet	
End:	12 05 27 698E	35 83 659N
End elevation:	7036 feet	
Projected Distance:	1.813 miles.	
	2.918 kilometers.	
Projected Area:	4250500 sq. feet	
	97.578 acres	
	0.394 sq. kilometers	

Options: => Profile... | => Route... | => Track...
Clear | Continue | Help

The distance from start to end is 1.83 miles. An area of 97.578 acres is enclosed in the route. © Maptech. Reproduced with permission.

or a search area can all easily be measured by taking a few coordinates from the area and feeding them to the computer.

Altitude Profiling

One of the best features of topographical databases is altitude profiling. After the user draws a route on the map, the computer instantly produces a cross-section showing all the changes in altitude along the path. Try profiling a trail on a paper map and you will see the power of this feature. Profiling allows you to see in advance which sections of

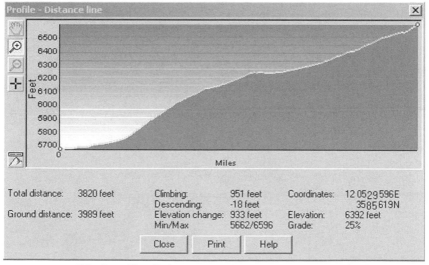

Total distance:	3820 feet	Climbing:	951 feet	Coordinates:	12 05 29 596E
		Descending:	-18 feet		35 85 619N
Ground distance:	3989 feet	Elevation change:	933 feet	Elevation:	6392 feet
		Min/Max	5662/6596	Grade:	25%

Close | Print | Help

Altitude profiling displays the vertical change along the planned trail. © Maptech.

the trail will be challenging and which will be easy. Some map programs can only generate a two-dimensional profile of a path that is useful to professionals who design trails, plan evacuation routes, etc. Other programs can provide 3-D relief pictures like those shown in Chapter 10. Guidebook writers can use a GPS receiver in the field to accurately mark the trail, then transfer the waypoints to the map database to calculate its length and profile, thereby making their maps accurate and informative.

Some map programs will show named points along the trail on the profile, which correlates the profile to places that are easily identifiable in the field.

Autoroute Generation

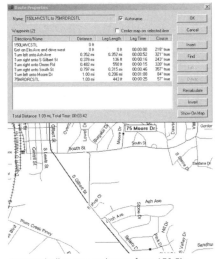

Computer based map programs combine a search engine with a route generation routine to provide a powerful tool for planning a trip. Imagine you want to go from your house to a place where you have never been before, but for which you have the address. You activate the Route function on the computer and select your house address. The computer searches the map, finds your address and uses your house as the starting waypoint for a route. Next you type in the address of the destination. The computer searches for the destination on the map, finds it and uses it as the last way-point in the route. The computer then determines the roads and the turns you need to make to get from your house to the destination. When the computer finishes calcu-lating the route, it has your house as the first point, the destination as the last point and a list of the roads you take to get from the start to the end.

Automatically generated route from 150 Elm Street to 75 Moore Street in Castle Rock, Colorado. © Garmin. Reproduced with permission.

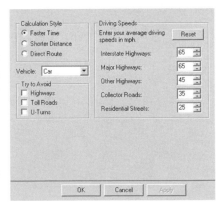

User selectable options for automatic route generation. © Garmin. Reproduced with permission.

172

You can influence how the computer selects the route between the start and the destination by having the computer select for faster time, shorter distance, using or avoiding highways, etc. Many programs allow you to type in the speed you generally travel for a specific type of road, whether it be interstate, highway or residential. The program uses the speeds you enter to calculate the amount of time it will take to travel the route generated by the computer.

Printing

There is no need to buy separate paper maps in addition to a map database program because maps can easily be printed from the database for use in the field. The user specifies the area to be printed, the scale, the amount of detail and if a grid is to appear on the print. User information added to the database can also appear on the printed version, so when you need to see the towers of the cellular phone network, the accidents in the metro area or a watershed's boundaries, the information is superimposed on the map. Even if you are in a situation where you can take a portable computer on your trip, printing out hard copies of the route is still important because in the case of computer failure, a backup plan is always important.

Presently map database programs can put a grid on the map. However, many times the grid is not directly usable for finding coordinates without additional preparation. All the techniques taught in the previous chapters will help you deal with whatever grid the database program produces. If you always print maps at the same scale, you can even make a ruler to quickly find coordinates. Fortunately, the map programs are improving daily and soon the grid on the map from your database program will be useful just as it is printed.

Downloadable Maps

If a receiver is capable of storing downloadable maps, it also has a computer program associated with it that displays the maps on the computer and enables you to select which maps will be transferred to the receiver for use in the field. Downloadable map programs have all the capabilities listed above for non-map and computer based map programs. They have search engines, waypoint marking, route calculation and many other features. The big difference is that the map you see on the computer screen, with all the waypoints and routes that you have marked, transfers to the receiver screen. The map shown on the computer is exactly the same map seen on the receiver when used in the field. Downloadable maps make paper maps obsolete, as long as your receiver is functioning properly. As you travel, you can watch your progress on the downloaded map and see all roads or mountains go by on the receiver's screen.

Downloadable map as seen on the computer screen. © Garmin. Reproduced with permission.

Obviously because of the difference in screen size, the computer will show more area with greater detail than the receiver; however, any street or geographical feature than can be seen on the computer can also be seen on the receiver screen if zoomed in properly. The important point with downloadable maps is that the information available on the computer can be downloaded onto the receiver and displayed in the field.

Generally, maps capable of being downloaded into a receiver are available only from the receiver manufacturer and they generally cost more than the computer-based map programs described earlier. If your use of a GPS receiver require downloadable maps, and especially if you plan on traveling in foreign countries, check with the manufacturer before you purchase to ensure that the maps you need are available.

14 PDAs, Pocket PCs, Laptops and Radios

GPS technology has been combined with Personal Digital Assistants (PDA), Pocket PCs, laptop computers, fish finders and radios. Soon, if it has not happened already, mobile phones will be GPS capable. Knowing where you are is very useful. The limits of where GPS technology will be applied are not known and new uses will continue to emerge. This chapter deals with some of the latest developments where GPS technology is combined with known technology.

Navman GPS receiver connected to a Palm M Series PDA to form a powerful navigation tool.

GPS and the Laptop Computer

GPS receivers have been capable of connecting to computers for several years. Mapping software for PCs has been available for about the same amount of time. Connecting your receiver to your laptop, so it can act as a moving road map in your car is nothing new, but what is new is the types of receivers developed specifically for use with laptop computers. Entire GPS receivers are manufactured in an external antenna. The receiver/antenna is placed on the roof of the car and the wire leading from it is connected to the PC. The antenna continuously sends position information to the PC, which displays your position on the laptop screen. These combination units are very small and convenient to use. No longer do you have to connect your much larger handheld receiver to your laptop.

GPS receivers for laptops also come in a PCMCIA form factor, which is convenient and small, but it may be difficult for the receiver to pick up the satellites while in the car. Current external antenna/GPS receiver combo models are the Garmin USB 35 TracPak and the Navman E Series for laptops.

GPS and Radios

Several years ago, the Family Radio Service (FRS) frequency was set aside for handheld radios that work over a short distance of approximately two miles. Soon small radios were available. Families and friends could stay in contact at the mall or while on an activity. Such radios are now available with an integrated GPS receiver. The radios have a display much like a normal handheld GPS receiver which shows your position and possibly a base map or downloadable map. The best part of the radios is that you can not only stay in touch with other people who have the radios, but you can see their position on your screen. In addition to sending voices between the radios, your position coordinate is also sent and is displayed on your friend's screen. You no longer have to use the radio to ask where the other members of your party are because you can see their position on your screen and they can see yours.

Garmin Rino 120 two-way radio integrated with a WAAS-enabled GPS receiver.

Integrated PDA-GPS Receiver

This section and the next describes how GPS receivers designed for Personal Digital Assistants (PDA) and Pocket PCs turn electronic organizers and mini-PCs into powerful navigation tools. GPS-PDA combinations come in two forms. In the first type the GPS receiver is an integral part of the PDA—it is not a PDA to which a GPS receiver has been bolted on. A single manufacturer produces integrated GPS-PDA devices at present. The other type of GPS-PDA devices have a GPS receiver that has to be connected to a PDA or Pocket PC. The GPS receivers are specially designed for the specific PDA or Pocket PC.

The integrated GPS-PDA looks like a normal PDA, but with an antenna. The PDA works much like any other PDA in that it has a calendar, address book, to do lists, memos, etc., but it also supports software that turns your PDA into a GPS receiver with great maps and a color screen.

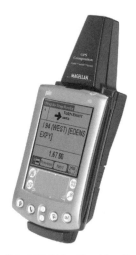

Palm 505 PDA with a Magellan Companion GPS receiver.

The capabilities of PDA based navigation systems are discussed in the next section.

GPS Combined with PDAs and Pocket PCs

GPS receivers of different sizes and shapes are available to turn your PDA or Pocket PC into a powerful GPS receiver with maps as good as any downloadable maps offered.

The Pocket PC is the latest development in computers. Both PDAs and Pocket PCs are specialized computers. Like regular computers, PDA and Pocket PC models vary in speed, amount of memory and processing power. The more powerful models can run mapping software that makes them comparable to the less expense GPS receivers designed specifically for vehicles. The mapping software allows the PDA or Pocket PC to do everything a handheld receiver can do plus automatic route calculation. They have the capabilities of mobile receivers in addition to being small enough to carry.

Garmin iQue 3600 integrated PDA displays an autorouted route.

Turning a Pocket PC into a GPS receiver requires:

- A specialized GPS receiver.
  No display, no waypoint memory.
  Connects to Pocket PC.
  Simply reports current position to the Pocket PC.

- A connector between the Pocket PC and GPS receiver.
  Wire connectors.
  Wireless Bluetooth connectors.
  Compact Flash (CF) inserted receivers.

- Mapping software for a Pocket PC.
  The Pocket PC runs the mapping software.
  Shows current position on a map.
  Remembers routes and waypoints.
  Provides automatically generated maps.

Garmin iQue 3600 integrates GPS and a PDA.

The GPS receivers for PDAs and Pocket PCs are not like the receivers shown and discussed in Chapter 4. The receiver that attaches to PDAs and Pocket PCs needs to have an antenna for receiving the satellite signals and the position calculation circuit required to calculate position from the incoming satellite signals. It does not have to have a screen, any memory to store waypoints or routes, or any capability aside from calculating its current position. In fact, the type of receiver required for PDAs and Pocket PCs is exactly the same as those described in the section above titled GPS and the Laptop Computer. The arrangement is exactly the same, except the PDA or Pocket PC replaces the laptop computer. The GPS receiver for PDAs and Pocket PCs operates exactly like a laptop receiver. The receiver continuously reports its current position and the PDA or Pocket PC keeps track of routes, waypoints Goto destination, speed calculations, direction, ETE or any other navigation statistic. The PDA or Pocket PC, in conjunction with the mapping software, is the brains of the navigation system. The PDA or Pocket PC does all the thinking and does everything necessary for navigation using the position reported by the GPS receiver.

PDA and Pocket PC navigation systems have advantages and disadvantages over traditional handheld GPS receivers.

Advantages

- Color screen if you want it.
- Larger than average screen.
- More memory to store waypoints, routes, track logs and maps.
- Greater variety of map programs available.
- Ability to automatically calculate routes using road map software.

Disadvantages

- Uses lots of batteries. Best used in a vehicle with cigarette lighter power.
- Not waterproof.
- Larger than smallest available handheld receivers.
- Higher cost.

Using a PDA or Pocket PC for navigation costs more than a traditional handheld because you have to buy the PDA or Pocket PC in addition to the GPS receiver and the navigation software. By far the greatest advantage of a PDA or Pocket PC based system is the availability of map programs. The PDAs and Pocket PCs support map programs from several manufacturers—not just the receiver manufacturer. It is also possible to get map programs from different vendors for different areas. If one map program is better in Europe and a different one in Australia, you can purchase and use the programs from both vendors. The PDA/Pocket PC system provides definite advantages when it comes to topographical maps. Downloadable topographical maps for handheld GPS receivers use 1:100,000 scale maps, whereas topographical maps for PDA/Pocket PCs use 1:24,000 scale maps, which provide much greater detail. Depending on the amount of memory in the PDA or Pocket PC, you can load multiple map programs and use the one that provides the best information for a specific location.

A Navman GPS with a Compaq iPAQ Pocket PC running Outdoor Navigator topographical map software from Maptech. Map scale is 1:24,000. © Maptech. Reproduced with permission.

Watch for developments in the area of PDA/Pocket PC combined with GPS receivers. The PDAs and Pocket PCs are only going to get more powerful, with more memory and greater processing power while the GPS receivers designed for them will get smaller. The day will arrive when maps of entire countries will fit on your PDA/Pocket PC and the GPS receiver will be a small unit, with a wireless connection, that can be placed just about anywhere.

Your navigation needs will determine if you can use a Pocket PC navigation system. Today, if you travel the backcountry, the weight and battery consumption may make a PDA/Pocket PC system less practical. If you travel via boat, plane or land vehicle and need detailed maps with a larger screen, the Pocket PC approach may be for you. If it is not for you today, it may be in a few years when they are smaller, lighter and use less power.

Marine charts are available for PDA/Pocket PC combinations. © Maptech. Reproduced with permission.

15 Other Grids

There are innumerable grids in addition to UTM and latitude/longitude. Some are limited to a single country or area like Universal Polar Stereographic or Ordnance Survey Great Britain. Even though most maps have latitude/longitude, it may be the secondary grid and the primary grid may be more convenient to use. If you think you will need a grid that is not UTM or latitude/longitude, be sure the receiver supports it before you buy. This chapter describes the basics of the following grids:

- Universal Polar Stereographic (UPS)
- Ordnance Survey Great Britain (OSGB)
- Military Grid Reference System (MGRS)
- Maidenhead

Universal Polar Stereographic (UPS)

The Universal Polar Stereographic (UPS) grid was developed to provide the Arctic and Antarctic regions with a uniform grid. The UTM grid can extend to cover the entire earth, but it can be confusing near the poles because the zones would be very narrow. Like UTM, the UPS grid has eastings and northings that form 1 km (0.62 mi.) squares. The UPS coordinates for both the north and south poles are given in the tables. Most receivers display the zone as 0. The Greenwich Meridian (0° longitude) and the International Date Line (W 180° longitude) form the zone meridian that references all easting measurements. The longitude lines W 90° and E 90° form the meridian for measuring northing coordinates. Some receivers use the MGRS letters Y and Z for the north pole and A and B for the south pole to label west and east of the easting meridian respectively. The number of points in the figure correspond to the coordinates listed below. There is a direct correspondence between the latitude/longitude grid and the UPS grid only at the meridians, but the tables include latitude/longitude for all the points to help you relate the UPS coordinate to a grid you already know.

Arctic UPS Coordinates

Point	lat/long	UPS Coordinate		
#1	N 84°, W 180°	0 Y	2000000m.E.	2666760m.N.
#2	N 88°, W 135°	0 Y	1842965m.E.	2157035m.N.
#3	N 84°, W 90°	0 Y	1333237m.E.	2000000m.N.
#4	N 88°, W 45°	0 Y	1842965m.E.	1842965m.N.
#5	N 84°, E 0°	0 Z	2000000m.E.	1333237m.N.
#6	N 88°, E 45°	0 Z	2157035m.E.	1842965m.N.
#7	N 84°, E 90°	0 Z	2666764m.E.	2000000m.N.
#8	N 88°, E 135°	0 Z	2157035m.E.	2157035m.N.
North Pole	N 90°	0 Z	2000000m.E.	2000000m.N.

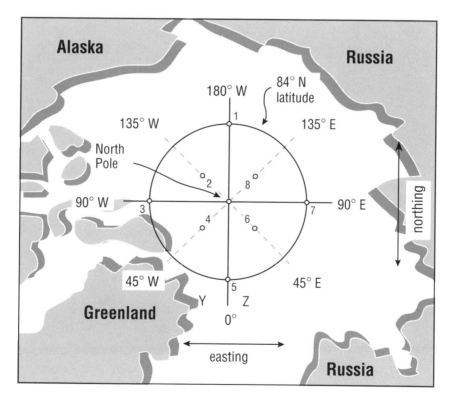

The Antarctic region is similar to the Arctic except the outer circle is S 80°. The figure shows how the UPS grid is laid out for the south pole and also gives the coordinates of some points.

Antarctic UPS Coordinates

Point	lat/long	UPS Coordinate	
#1	S 80°, W 180°	0 A 2000000m.E.	886989m.N.
#2	S 85°, W 135°	0 A 1607211m.E.	1607211m.N.
#3	S 80°, W 90°	0 A 886989m.E.	2000000m.N.
#4	S 85°, W 45°	0 A 1607211m.E.	2392789m.N.
#5	S 80°, E 0°	0 B 2000000m.E.	3113011m.N.
#6	S 85°, E 45°	0 B 2392789m.E.	2392789m.N.
#7	S 80°, E 90°	0 B 3113011m.E.	2000000m.N.
#8	S 85°, E 135°	0 B 2392789m.E.	1607311m.N.
South Pole S 90°		0 B 2000000m.E.	2000000m.N.

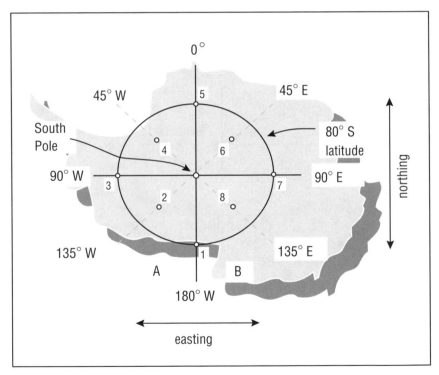

Ordnance Survey Great Britain (OSGB)

The Ordnance Survey Great Britain is a national grid that covers only Great Britain. The country is divided into 100 km (62.1 mi.) square sections (100 km x 100 km) that are lettered with two letters as shown in the figure. Each section is divided into 1 km squares. The grid uses easting and northing numbers to describe locations like the UTM grid. A large scale map (1:25,000 or 1:50:000) covers only a portion of the 100 km section.

				HP			
HQ	HR	HS	HT	HU	JQ		
HV	HW	HX	HY	HZ	JV		
NA	NB	NC	ND	NE	OA		
NF	NG	NH	NJ	NK	OF		
NL	NM	NN	NO	NP	OL		
NQ	NR	NS	NT	NU	OQ		
	NW	NX	NY	NZ	OV		
	SB	SC	SD	SE	TA		
	SG	SH	SJ	SK	TF	TG	
	SM	SN	SO	SP	TL	TM	
SQ	SR	SS	ST	SU	TQ	TR	
SV	SW	SX	SY	SZ	TV		

Eastings and Northings

OSGB easting and northing coordinates are much like UTM:

- Increasing easting numbers means you are going east.
- Increasing northing numbers means you are going north.
- Full coordinate is 440000m, 457000m.
- The large numbers shown on a map are an abbreviation. For example: 40 means 440000m and 57 means 457000m.
- Distance between **40** and **41** is 1000 m (1 km).
- The last three numbers stand for meters.
- Distance between 339000m and 339541m is 541 m.

OSGB Coordinates

- An OSGB coordinate is section letters, easting and northing.
- The section is printed on the map. A typical value is SE.
- When the section is specified, omit the small number in front.
- An OSGB coordinate would be written as: SE **38**000m, **57**900m.
- It may also be shown abbreviated as: SE **38**0 **57**9
- Eastings and northings are not marked m.E. and m.N.
- When using a GPS receiver, the full coordinate: section letters, easting and northing, must be used. Abbreviations are too map specific.

If you travel in Great Britain and use your GPS receiver, you will find the OSGB grid is much easier to use than the latitude/longitude grid because the 1 km (0.62 mi.) squares are printed on the map. On large scale maps, it is possible to read coordinates directly from the grid. However, if you prefer to use a ruler, you can use any of those introduced in the UTM grid chapters if you have the correct scale.

Military Grid Reference System (MGRS)

Most outdoor enthusiasts do not use the MGRS grid because USGS topographical maps do not provide it. However, if you prefer the MGRS grid, see Chapter 13. Electronic map databases will print a map with the MGRS grid. MGRS is simply a modified form of the UTM grid where the first two numbers of the easting and northing are replaced with letters. It is a lot like the OSGB grid because the letters are assigned to 100 km x 100 km squares.

The UTM and MGRS coordinates for the same location are shown below. The first two numbers of the easting and northing were converted to the letters "WB." The 05 from the easting became the "W" while the 36 from the northing became "B." The m.E. and m.N. were removed. All the other numbers remain the same. Sometimes MGRS coordinates are written as a continuous string of numbers and letters as shown on the last line, but most GPS receivers keep the zone designator, the easting and northing separate, so everything is legible.

UTM:	12 S	05**01**788m.E. 36**90**619m.N.
MGRS:	12 S	WB 01788, 90619
	12 SWB 0178890619	

Much like any other grid, GPS receivers require you to enter all the numbers of each coordinate, which means a position is specified down to 1 m. The two tables below can be used to convert from UTM to MGRS, but if you ever have a full UTM coordinate and need to convert it to MGRS, simply enter the UTM coordinate into the receiver and let it do the conversion.

Converting the Easting Number

Some receivers do not show the easting coordinate with a leading zero. The table below assumes a leading zero. To use the table, find the zone to the right and the first digits of the easting at the top and where they intersect is the letter that replaces the easting digits. For example, if you were in zone 47 and the first two numbers of the easting is 03, the numbers 03 would be replaced by the letter "L."

Easting	01	02	03	04	05	06	07	08	Zone
	S	T	U	V	W	X	Y	Z	3, 6, 9, 12, 15, 18, 21, 24, 27, 30, 33, 36, 39, 42, 45, 48, 51, 54, 57, 60
	J	K	L	M	N	P	Q	R	2, 5, 8, 11, 14, 17, 20, 23, 26, 29, 32, 35, 38, 41, 44, 47, 50, 53, 56, 59
	A	B	C	D	E	F	G	H	1, 4, 7, 10, 13, 16, 19, 22, 25, 28, 31, 34, 37, 40, 43, 46, 49, 52, 55, 58

Converting the Northing Number

The first two digits of the northing number are converted to a letter by finding the leading two digits at the bottom of the table and the zone number to the right and where they intersect is the letter that replaces the northing digits. If the zone were 34 and the first digits of the northing 03, the northing numbers would be converted to a letter as follows: The first digit of the northing number is 0, which is even, so you would look at the left half of the table in the section "Even first northing digit." The second northing digit is 3, so you would select the column in the even section that has a 3, which is the fourth column over from the left side of the table. The zone, 34, is even, so you would select the upper row of letters to get the letter "J" to replace the first two digits of the northing number. A few examples are given below to help learn to use the tables if you want to convert from UTM to MGRS or vice versa by hand.

																					Zone
F	G	H	J	K	L	M	N	P	Q	R	S	T	U	V	A	B	C	D	E		Even
A	B	C	D	E	F	G	H	J	K	L	M	N	P	Q	R	S	T	U	V		Odd
0	1	2	3	4	5	6	7	8	9	0	1	2	3	4	5	6	7	8	9		
Even first northing digit										Odd first northing digit											

UTM:	56 S	03**46**629m.E.	37**84**395m.N.
MGRS:	56 S	LC 46629	84395

UTM:	19 V	05**13**897m.E.	66**36**786m.N.
MGRS:	19 V	EG 13897	36786

Maidenhead Grid

The Maidenhead grid was developed and is used by amateur radio operators. It divides the world into grids with dimensions 20° of longitude by 10° of latitude, which are identified by two letters, AA-RR. The grids are subdivided into areas 2°x 1° and labeled with two numbers 00-99. The areas are further subdivided into sub-areas that are 5' of longitude by 2.5' of latitude and labeled with letters AA-XX. A Maidenhead coordinate looks like this: EM18BX.

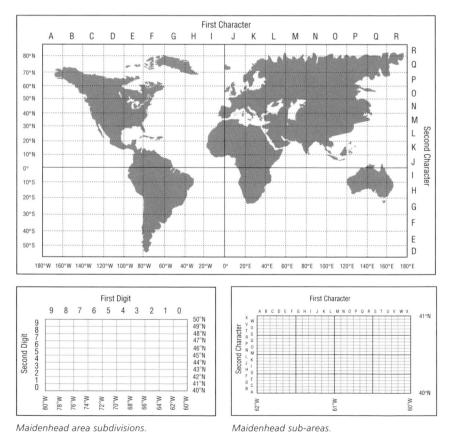

Maidenhead area subdivisions.   *Maidenhead sub-areas.*

16 Differential GPS and WAAS

The Wide Area Augmentation System (WAAS) was introduced in Chapter 1. As you know by now, WAAS makes a receiver accurate to 3 m (9.8 ft.) 95% of time. This chapter explains how WAAS works and also explains the principles of Differential GPS (DGPS) because WAAS is simply a form of DGPS.

Just as the name sounds, Differential GPS uses the difference between two measurements to improve the accuracy of GPS position calculations. DGPS can be used to increase accuracy to 2 mm (0.79 in.) when necessary, but as you can imagine, greater accuracy means extra equipment and increased cost. DGPS uses two methods to increase position calculations:

- **Real-time corrections**

  Corrections made in the field while moving. WAAS is based on real-time corrections.

- **Post-processed corrections**

  Corrections made in the office after the trip. Not good for navigation.

Real-Time Corrections

Real-time corrections are used for navigation in the field. The figure on the next page illustrates how real-time DGPS works. The captain of a ship has entered an unknown port. His chart shows there is a large underwater rock somewhere in the lane. He needs to avoid the rock or it will sink his ship, but try as he might, he cannot see any marking buoys. Fortunately, the captain has a GPS receiver that can receive differential corrections, which means his receiver can provide positions calculations more accurate than the 15 m (49.2 ft.) accuracy the GPS provides without differential corrections.

On a hill nearby, a DGPS site has a receiver and a radio transmitter. The GPS receiver at the DGPS site continuously calculates its position, yet it never moves. The DGPS site was built on an accurately surveyed spot, so the site computer knows its position regardless of what the GPS receiver reports. When the receiver reports a position of (x+3, y-5), the site computer knows that its true position, via the survey, is (x, y). The site computer takes the position calculated by the GPS receiver and compares it to its known position. The difference, the result from the comparison, is the amount the GPS receiver's position is in error. In this case, the receiver's position error is +3 units in the x direction and -5 units in the y direction. Once the site knows the receiver's position error, it uses its radio to broadcast correction information. Any receiver that can pick up the radio wave, like the receiver on the boat, can use the correction information to make its own position calculation more accurate. In this example, if the GPS receiver on the boat reports a position of (x+34, y+60), it uses the DGPS information to correct its position to (x+31, y+65). The corrections allow the captain's receiver to know how much error is present in its position calculation and to remove that error.

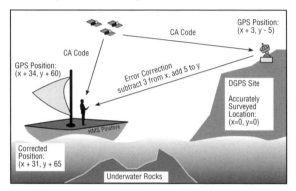

DGPS, available in most U.S. ports, increases civilian receiver accuracy.

Usually DGPS is accurate over a limited area of approximately 274 km (170 mi.) because if your position is too far from the DGPS site, the data may not be for the same satellites as those used by your receiver to calculate its position. Most DGPS signals are also broadcast over the Loran-C frequency, which requires you to purchase a Loran-C antenna and a special DGPS receiver box to connect to your GPS receiver. This enables you to pickup and use the correction radio broadcast. The DGPS corrections are sent in the RTCM format, so if you want to be able to use DGPS, be sure your receiver accepts the RTCM format. Although the U.S. Coast Guard has set up DGPS sites throughout the U.S., DGPS, for most outdoor users, has been overshadowed by WAAS.

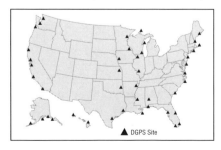

DGPS sites set up by the US Coast Guard currently cover waterways.

WAAS

The Wide Area Augmentation System (WAAS) is a GPS-based navigation and landing system that provides precision guidance to aircraft at thousands of airports and airstrips where there is currently no precision landing capability. It is a form of differentially corrected GPS and is designed to improve the accuracy and ensure the integrity of information coming from GPS satellites. There are land stations across the U.S. that determine the amount of error for any GPS satellite at any time. The corrections are calculated and up-linked to two WAAS satellites that beam them to the continental U.S. and Alaska where WAAS enabled receivers use the correction information to make their calculated position more accurate. WAAS testing in September 2002 confirmed accuracy performance of 1 – 2 meters horizontal and 2 –3 meters vertical throughout the majority of the continental U.S. and portions of Alaska.

WAAS is called wide area because it's signal is broadcast and is usable over a wide area. The great thing about WAAS is that it broadcasts on the same frequencies used by GPS satellites (L1 and L2), so a receiver does not have to have any additional equipment to receive WAAS corrections.

WAAS is free if you buy a WAAS enabled receiver. Most receivers are WAAS enabled, so 3 m (9.8 ft.) accuracy is available without additional cost or inconvenience anywhere in the continental U.S. and Alaska. WAAS coverage will be extended to Hawaii and Canada in the near future.

Other governments are developing similar satellite-based differential systems. The European system is EGNOS (Euro Geostationary Navigation Overlay Service). The Japanese are developing MSAS (Multi-Functional Satellite Augmentation System). Receivers that pick up the WAAS satellites should be able to access these other systems when they become functional.

Post-Processed Corrections

Just as the name implies, post-processing corrections are not applied in the field, but in the office after the trip is over. Consumer grade receivers do not collect the information necessary to apply post-processed corrections. Professionals who need a method to generate accurate positions, but do not want to spend the money for real-time, highly accurate DGPS systems will still be interested in post-processing. Outdoor enthusiasts can be happy that WAAS gives them more accuracy than has previously available. And at the right price.

Local Area DGPS

Localized DGPS has not been eliminated by WAAS. The U.S. Coast Guard operates over 60 DGPS sites along U.S. coasts, the Great Lakes, Puerto Rico, parts of Alaska and Hawaii. The organization is also developing a ground-based system to provide coverage across the entire continental U.S.

The Coast Guard system requires the user to purchase an antenna and a DGPS unit in addition to a DGPS enabled receiver. Most outdoor users will not be interested in the Coast Guard system because WAAS is more convenient; however, other countries like Norway, Sweden, Finland and the Netherlands have established DGPS sites comparible to the U.S. system. If you travel the oceans, you may want to buy the equipment necessary to receive DGPS RTCM transmissions because DGPS may be available in a country where WAAS is not available.

The U.S. Federal Aviation Administration is developing a system for aircraft landings at small- and medium-sized airports called the Local Area Augmentation System (LAAS). It operates on an area within a 20-30 mile radius, broadcasting a correction message via a VHF radio data link from a ground-based transmitter. LAAS has a demonstrated accuracy of less than 1 meter in both the horizontal and vertical axis which will provide the neccessary accuracy for Category I, II, and III precision approaches.

One fascinating application of DGPS equipment is to track the movements of hydrological dams. You might question the need of tracking the movements of a dam that holds back a lake of water. You might think that visual inspection could settle the question as to the dam's location and that proper operation will brevent a dam from collapsing. All those observations are correct, but still, highly accurate DGPS makes it possible to track the movement of a dam down to a few millimeters. As the lake fills with water, the DGPS equipment can report how much the dam has flexed and allows the operators to keep the water levels and the fill rate below the failure point of the dam.

17 Degrees, Minutes, Seconds and Mils

The circle is an important part of navigation because once the circle on the compass is oriented correctly, you can orient yourself and travel in the right direction. How the circle is subdivided into degrees, minutes, seconds and mils is described below. How to do arithmetic using these units is also demonstrated.

Relating Degrees, Minutes and Seconds to Each Other

In order to understand latitude/longitude or bearings, you need to understand how degrees, minutes, seconds and mils are related. The equator wraps around the entire earth and forms a circle that is the basis of degrees, minutes, seconds and mils. If you want to talk about only part of the circle, it must be subdivided. The most common subdivision of a circle is called the degree. The unit of mils is another way to subdivide the circle, but it will be discussed after degrees, minutes and seconds are explained. There are 360° in a circle. A part of a circle can be expressed as degrees. A half circle is 180°, a quarter is 90°, and so forth.

The degree is subdivided into minutes. There are 60' (the single tick mark is the symbol for minutes) in a degree. Minutes are also subdivided into seconds and following a familiar pattern, there are 60" (the symbol for seconds is two tick marks) in a minute. The relationships between degrees, minutes and seconds are as follows:

$$1 \text{ full circle} = 360°$$
$$1° = 60' = 3,600"$$
$$1' = 60"$$

When adding degrees, remember to wrap around from 359° to 0° and when subtracting, 0° is followed by 359°. It is possible to have more than 360°, but it just means you have turned full circle and then some more. For example, 526° is simply a full circle of 360° plus an additional 166° as shown in the figure on the next page.

When a bearing is greater than 360°, simply subtract 360 until the result is less than 360° and that is the direction you should go. For example, if you are told to walk a bearing of 810°, you would do the following math:

$810° - 360° = 450°$
$450° - 360° = 90°$

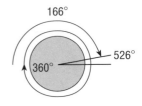

The result shows that the bearing 810° is really just 90°, which is due east as shown in the figure opposite.

Adding and Subtracting Minutes and Seconds

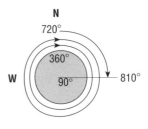

When working with minutes and seconds, the value wraps from 59 to 0 and 0 to 59 when adding and subtracting respectively, but in these cases, either the degrees or minutes is also affected, so you have to keep track of them. Here are a few examples:

45" + 20" = 65"	= 60" + 5"	= 1' 5"
23' + 58' = 81'	= 60' + 21'	= 1° 21'
5' 19" − 20" = 4' (60" + 19") − 20"	= 4' 79" − 20"	= 4' 59"
56° 25' − 47' = 55° (60' + 25') − 47'	= 55° 85' − 47'	= 55° 38'

82° 45' 23" − 56' 43"
  = 82° 44' (60" + 23") - 56' 43"
  = 82° 44' 83" − 56' 43"
  = 81° (60' + 44') 83" − 56' 43"
  = 81° 104' 83" − 56' 43"
  = 81° (104' − 56') (83" − 43")
  = 81° 48' 40"

Adding/Subtracting Degrees and Minutes

The same care with minutes must be taken when the format is degrees and minutes as demonstrated in the examples below:

219° 19.42' + 36.81'
  = 219° (19.42' + 36.81')
  = 219° 56.23'

61° 27.46' − 53.41'
  = 60° (60' + 27.46') − 53.41'
  = 60° 87.46' − 53.41'
  = 60° 34.05'

The use of degrees only eliminates all the work required to keep track of minutes and seconds, but you still need to remember there are 360° in a circle.

46.492° - 21.613° = 24.879°

105.386° - 283.426°
  = (360° + 105.386°) - 283.426°
  = 465.386° - 283.426°
  = 181.96°

315.395° + 284.305° = 599.7°
  = 599.7° - 360°
  = 239.7°

Converting Degrees to Degrees and Minutes

Another requirement to become proficient is the ability to convert from degrees to degrees and minutes. The transformation is done as follows.

57.146° = 57° (0.146 x 60')
  = 57° 8.76'

357.963° = 357° (0.963 x 60')
  = 357° 57.78'

Converting Degrees to Degrees, Minutes and Seconds

Conversion from degrees to degrees, minutes and seconds is similar to the above translation with one additional step.

295.248° = 295° (0.248 x 60')
  = 295° 14.88'
  = 295° 14' (0.88 x 60")
  = 295° 14' 52.8"

136.389° = 136° (0.389 x 60')
  = 136° 23.34'
  = 136° 23' (0.34 x 60")
  = 136° 23' 20.4"

Converting Seconds to Minutes

The conversion of degrees, minutes and seconds to degrees and minutes is also important. Seconds are converted to minutes by multiplying by 1'/60". Remember from above that 1' is equal to 60", so the term 1'/60" is really just equal to one. This means you are multiplying the seconds by a number with a value of 1, so its value does not change, but it allows the units to convert from seconds to minutes. The example below explicitly shows the number's units.

$$39" \times [1'/60"] = \frac{39" \times 1'}{60"}$$

The seconds unit of the 39" on top cancel out with the seconds unit of the 60" on the bottom. The equation becomes:

$$\frac{39 \times 1'}{60} \quad \text{The final value becomes} \quad \frac{39}{60} \times 1' = (0.65) \times 1' = 0.65'$$

The examples below demonstrate conversion from degrees, minutes and seconds to degrees and minutes. The units are not explicitly shown, but just remember that when seconds are divided by 60, they become minutes.

105° 47' 51" = 105° (47 + [51/60])'
= 105° (47 + 0.85)'
= 105° 47.85'
326° 9' 32.4" = 326° (9 + [32.4/60])'
= 326° (9 + 0.54)'
= 326° 9.54'

Converting Minutes to Degrees

The conversion from degrees and minutes to degrees requires minutes to be converted to degrees. Minutes are converted to degrees by multiplying by 1°/60'. As with the previous case, 1° is equal to 60', so multiplying by the term 1°/60' does not change the value of the minutes, it simply converts the unit from minutes to degrees. The units are explicitly shown below:

$$46' \times [1°/60'] = \frac{46' \times 1°}{60'}$$

The minutes unit of the 46' on top cancel out with the minutes unit of the 60' on the bottom and the equation becomes:

$\dfrac{46 \times 1°}{60}$ The final value becomes $\dfrac{46}{60} \times 1° = (0.767) \times 1° = 0.767°$

The examples below demonstrate conversion from degrees and minutes to degrees. The units are not explicitly shown, but just as it was shown above, when minutes are divided by 60, they become degrees.

261° 36' = (261 + [36/60])°
= (261 + 0.6)°
= 261.6°

57° 41.475' = (57 + [41.475/60])°
= (57 + 0.691)°
= 57.691°

Converting Degrees, Minutes and Seconds to Degrees

Take all the conversion knowledge acquired and convert degrees, minutes and seconds to degrees.

269° 42' 35" = 269° (42 + [35/60])'
= 269° 42.583'
= (269 + [42.583/60])°
= 269.71°

48° 37' 3.4" = 48° (37 + [3.4/60])'
= 48° 37.057'
= (48 + [37.057/60])°
= 48.618°

Finding the Opposite Direction

The opposite direction to any bearing can be found by simply adding or subtracting 180°. Obvious opposites are E at 90° and W at 270°, which have a difference between them of 180°. The other examples shown below reiterate what to do when addition results in a bearing over 360° or less than 0°. Just remember that adding or subtracting 180° provides the same result, so do whichever results in the easiest math.

271° 15' 39" + 180° = (271 + 180)° 15' 39"
= 451° 15' 39"
= (451 - 360)° 15' 39"
= 91° 15' 39"

271° 15' 39" - 180° = (271 - 180)° 15' 39"
= 91° 15' 39"

23° 43' 9" - 180 = (23 - 180)° 43' 9"
= ([23 + 360] - 180)° 43' 9"
= (383 - 180)° 43' 9"
= 203° 43' 9"

23° 43' 9" + 180 = (23 + 180)° 43' 9"
= 203° 43' 9"

How Mils Relate to Degrees

There is more than one way to subdivide a circle. The degrees subdivision is the most common unit on maps, but mils are also used and should be understood. A mil is one sixty-four hundredth (1/6400) of a circle. The mil has the advantage that there are no conversions between units like minutes and seconds and it is also a finer division of the circle as there are only 3600" in a circle. For most navigators, the best use of the mil is to know how the mil relates to the degree. That relationship is listed below:

$$1 \text{mil} = \frac{360°}{6400} = 0.05625°$$

$$1° = \frac{6400 \text{ mils}}{360} = 17.778 \text{ mils}$$

To convert from degrees to mils, multiply the number of degrees by 17.778. To convert from mils to degrees, multiply the number of mils by 0.05625.

A few examples of equivalent mils and degrees are given below.

0° = 0 mils
90° = 1,600 mils
180° = 3,200 mils
270° = 4,800 mils

Receiver Classes

Dividing a receiver into classes may help you select a receiver that suites your needs. Categorizing receivers is highly subjective; however, sorting receivers into four broad categories provides a general guideline.

Basic Provides current position, stores waypoints, maybe has 1 route, possibly makes a track log, possibly connects to a computer to transfer waypoints. Definitely does not have a base map or support downloadable maps. Good for hiking or other activities on foot where a paper map is the primary means of navigation. Possibly WAAS enabled. Provides few navigational statistics. Garmin Geko 101& GPS 12 XL, Magellan 310.

Mid Range Has at least one route. Keeps a track log. Provides some navigational statistics. Most likely connects to a computer. May have a limited base map, but may not accept downloadable maps. If it does accept downloadable maps, its memory is small can cannot hold much area. Does support an external antenna. Good for pedestrians, can be used in boats or cars where a paper map provides the primary information about the area. WAAS enabled. Brunton Multi-Navigator, Garmin Geko 201, eTrex & Venture, Magellan Sportrak & Sportrak Map.

Upper Range Multiple routes. Has a good base map. Supports downloadable maps, but cannot automatically generate routes. Has more than minimal memory for maps or accepts memory sticks for map storage. Definitely connects to a computer. Provides a full range of navigational statistics. WAAS Enabled. On screen maps can be used as the primary information of an area. Useful in any means of travel. Probably has a electronic barometer, electronic altimeter and an electronic compass. Garmin eTrex Legend & Summit, Lowrance iFinder, Magellan Sportrak Pro

Top Range Everything that an Upper Range model has plus more. More memory, downloadable maps of a larger area, ability to automatically generate a route using its internal or downloaded map information. Possibly a color screen. Garmin eTrex Vista & GPSmap 76S, Magellan Meridian Platinum & Meridian Color.

Also available are:

Automotive GPS Systems Capable of automatic route generation and giving turn-by-turn instructions. Garmin Street Pilot III, Navman iCN-630, Magellan 750 Nav+ & 750 Nav M.

PDA/Pocket PC Receivers (also requires a PDA or Pocket PC and mapping software). Navman, Pharos.

Glossary

2D Mode. Position calculations in two dimensions. In terms of a GPS receiver, it means the receiver can lock on to only 3 satellites, so it cannot provide altitude. There may be substantial error in the horizontal coordinate it does provide.

3D Mode. Position calculations in three dimensions. The GPS receiver has locked on to 4 satellites. It provides an altitude in addition to a horizontal coordinate.

Almanac Data. Satellite position information. Each satellite broadcasts the position information for all the satellites. The receiver stores the information, so it can determine its own position. It takes about 12.5 minutes for the satellites to transfer the position data to the receiver.

Altimeter. A device that measures distance above sea level. Atmospheric pressure decreases as you rise in altitude, so most altimeters measure atmospheric pressure and relate it to height above sea level.

Antenna. A receiver needs an antenna to pick up the satellite signals beamed down from space. There are two common types for handheld receivers: patch (microstrip) and quadrifilar helix. The antenna is one of the most important components of a receiver. A remote antenna is separate from the antenna built into the receiver and is usually connected to the receiver by a cable. An active remote antenna is one that amplifies the satellite signals before sending them through the cable to the receiver.

Anti-Spoofing. It is possible to confuse GPS receivers by transmitting signals that look similar to the real satellite signals. Such an attack is known as spoofing. The military countermeasure is to encrypt the P code so only authorized users can recognize it and can detect and reject faked signals.

Azimuth. The direction of travel or the direction between two points in reference to true or magnetic north. When expressed in degrees, its value ranges from 0° to 360°. A compass heading is an azimuth. In most places, the word bearing has grown to mean the same thing as azimuth. See bearing.

Bearing. A bearing is your direction of travel or the direction between two points. Like an azimuth, a bearing is measured in reference to true or magnetic north, but its value never goes over 90°. A bearing is always measured from the cardinal directions north or south. A typical bearing would be N45°E, which is the same as an azimuth of 45°. The bearing S45°W is an azimuth of 225°. The use of the word bearing has changed over the years and now means the same thing as azimuth.

Bluetooth. Bluetooth enables electronic devices to communicate without wires. It is a short-range radio system. The communicating electronic devices must both have Bluetooth circuits to transmit and receiver signals. The main advantage is that there is no wire to get in the way. Bluetooth devices have a range of about 10 m (32.8 ft.).

Channel. The part of the GPS receiver's electronics that tunes in on a satellite's signal and sends the resulting information to the receiver's processor for position calculation.

Chart. A map of waterways or airways.

Coarse Acquisition Codes. The GPS satellites send two distinct signals: precision codes (P codes) and coarse acquisition codes (CA codes). Civilian receivers use the CA codes to determine position. Military receivers use the CA codes to synchronize to the P codes before switching to the use of P codes exclusively. Selective Availability used to affect the CA codes and thereby the accuracy of civilian receivers. The CA codes are transmitted on only one radio frequency, so it is impossible for a civilian receiver to detect the delay through the ionosphere. The accuracy provided by the CA codes is called the Standard Positioning Service (SPS).

Codeless Receivers. A class of GPS receivers that do not use the P codes or the CA codes to determine position. Codeless receivers measure the change in modulation in the satellite radio waves. They use sophisticated signal processing techniques to make position measurements accurate to centimeters. It can take days to make a single measurement.

Cold Start. A receiver experiences a cold start when it has to download the almanac information from the satellites before it can begin to calculate its own position. Refer to Time to First Fix.

Coordinate. The numbers and letters that describe a position. Every position on earth has a unique coordinate. The coordinate system determines the grid and how the coordinate is written.

Course. The path between two points. GPS receivers always indicate the straight line between two points.

Course Deviation Indicator (CDI). A method for displaying the amount and direction of CrossTrack error (XTE).

Course Made Good (CMG). The bearing from your starting point to your present position.

Course Over Ground (COG). Same as Course Made Good (CMG).

CrossTrack Error (XTE). The distance between your present position and the straight-line course between two points. It is the amount you are off the desired track (DTK).

Declination. The difference, in degrees or mils, between the north pole and the magnetic pole from your position. Many receivers have tables in their memory that tell them the amount and direction of declination for any position on earth, which means the receiver, once locked to the satellites, can automatically convert true north bearings to magnetic bearings and vice versa.

Degree. A part of a circle. The degree divides the circle into 360 even pieces. Bearings are also expressed in degrees. Degrees are subdivided into 60 minutes, which in turn are split into 60 second intervals.

DGPS Ready. A receiver is DGPS ready if it is capable of accepting Differential GPS correction data and using it to make its own position calculation more accurate. Additional equipment must be connected to the receiver to pick up the correction radio transmissions.

Differential GPS (DGPS). A method of improving civilian receiver accuracy. DGPS can be accurate to 15 m and below. DGPS corrections can be made instantaneously (real-time) as you are traveling or after the trip on stored waypoints (post-processing).

Dilution of Precision (DOP). An analysis of the satellite geometry and its impact on accuracy. Some satellite geometries provide more accurate position calculations. The receiver measures several factors that dilute the position accuracy and adds them all together to estimate how much error is present in its position calculation. Components of the DOP are horizontal, vertical, position and time dilutions of precision. A low value for a DOP means the receiver can accurately make a position calculation. A high value means there is increasingly more error in the position reported. Good DOP values range between 1 and 3. Most receivers will not even try to calculate position if the DOP values are greater than 6.

Easting. The distance east or west from the zone meridian. Easting coordinates are used in several grid systems. UTM, OSGB and MGRS are a few.

Ephemeris. The path and orbit information for a specific satellite. Selective Availability used to truncate the ephemeris information to limit the civilian receiver's accuracy.

Estimated Position Error (EPE). Many receivers report the potential error of a position calculation. The receiver knows the satellite geometry, and using the DOP values it estimates the amount of error that may be present in the position it calculates.

Estimated Time En Route (ETE). The amount of time remaining to arrive at the destination. ETE depends on the speed you are going directly toward the destination, which is called Velocity Made Good (VMG). If you are traveling away from the destination, the ETE cannot be calculated because you will never arrive.

Estimated Time of Arrival (ETA). The time of the day of arrival at the destination. ETA depends on the speed you are going directly toward the destination, which is called Velocity Made Good (VMG). If you are traveling away from the destination, the ETA cannot be calculated because you will never arrive.

Global Positioning System (GPS). A system of 24 satellites that allows a GPS receiver to determine its position any place in the world. There are two types of receivers: military and civilian. Military receivers are always accurate to about 1 m (3.3 ft.). Civilian receivers

were made less accurate by Selective Availability, but now that it has been removed, they are accurate to at least 15 m (49.2 ft.).

GLONASS. The Russian equivalent of the U.S. GPS. Its full name is Global'naya Navigatsionnaya Sputnikovaya Sistema.

Goto Function. A mode of operation where the receiver guides you to a destination. You must have previously stored the destination's coordinate in the receiver's memory. The receiver uses the satellite signals to find its present position, then it calculates the bearing and distance to the destination. In the Goto mode, the receiver usually displays a screen that points the direction you need to travel to arrive at the destination.

Greenwich Mean Time (GMT). The time as measured from Greenwich, England or 0° longitude. Refer to Universal Time Coordinated.

Grid. The horizontal and vertical lines on a map that fix your position. There are a lot of different grid systems because there are many different ways of translating a position from a sphere to a flat map. The most common grid systems are Universal Transverse Mercator (UTM) and latitude/longitude.

Grid North. The orientation of a map's grid. Cartographers try to align the vertical lines on the map with true north. However, there is usually a small difference between grid north and true north across the map, but the difference is so slight that it can usually be ignored for land navigation.

Ground Speed. Your speed across the ground regardless of direction. The speedometer in a car measures ground speed.

Heading. The direction of travel expressed as either a magnetic or true north bearing.

Glossary

Horizontal Dilution of Precision (HDOP). See Dilution of Precision.

Ionosphere. A layer of the earth's atmosphere between 50 and 250 mi. above the surface. The GPS satellite signals are delayed as they pass through the ionosphere. If the effect of the delay is not removed or compensated, the receiver's position calculation is inaccurate.

L1 and L2. The P code is transmitted on two radio frequencies known as L1 and L2. They are 1575.42 MHz and 1227.6 MHz respectively. The CA codes are transmitted only on the L1 frequency.

Landmark. Same as a waypoint. It can also refer to a distinct landform that is easily recognizable.

Latitude/Longitude. A spherical coordinate system. The lines of latitude and longitude form a grid system used to fix position. Latitude lines run parallel to the equator and measure distance from the equator while longitude lines are drawn from pole to pole and measure distance from the prime meridian in Greenwich, England (0°). Coordinates are measured in degrees, minutes or seconds.

Local Area Augmentation System (LAAS). A real-time DGPS corrections system being developed by the U.S. Federal Aviation Administration for use around airports. It will provide greater GPS accuracy than WAAS.

Lock. A receiver is locked when it can detect three or more satellites and it can use their signals to determine its own position.

Magnetic Declination. See Declination.

Magnetic North. The direction the compass needle points. A compass needle always points toward the magnetic pole located in northern Canada on Bathhurst Island. The magnetic pole is not the north pole.

Man-Overboard (MOB). A GPS receiver function that allows you to quickly mark a position in an emergency

Map Datum. All maps are drawn with respect to a reference point. The reference point is called the datum. Most map datum only cover a portion of the earth, like the North American Datum of 1927 (NAD 27), which covers only the continent of North America. The GPS makes it possible to have a worldwide datum like the World Geodetic System of 1984 (WGS 84).

Map Scales. The scale of a map is usually expressed in the form 1:24,000. The scale means that every inch on the map represents 24,000 inches on the ground. A large-scale map is one that is zoomed in; whereas, a small-scale map covers a lot of area on a single page.

Meridian. A longitude line that is used as a reference. The longitude line through Greenwich, England is referred to as the prime meridian and is labeled 0°. All other longitude lines are measured in relation to the prime meridian. Each zone in the UTM system also has a zone meridian used as the reference point for all east-west measurements.

Mil. A part of a circle. A mil is one part of a circle that is divided into 6400 equal-sized pieces.

Military Grid Reference System (MGRS). The grid system used by the U.S. military. It is similar to UTM except it replaces the most significant digits of the easting and northing numbers with letters. Some mapping programs will put the MGRS grid on USGS topographical maps for use by civilians.

Multipath. When the same signal from a satellite enters a receiver's antenna from more than one direction, it is called multipath. Usually the radio waves travel straight from the satellite to the receiver, but if it happens to bounce off some hard object, then it will enter both as a direct signal and as a reflected signal.

National Maritime Electronics Association (NMEA). NMEA protocols (how data is sent and what format it uses) specify the type and order of data sent and received by navigation equipment. If two pieces of equipment use the same NMEA protocol, they will understand each other and will operate together.

Navstar. Navstar Global Positioning System was the original name for the navigation system, but the Navstar part was soon lost and it is known today only as GPS. See Global Positioning System.

Northing. The distance north or south of a fixed reference point. The UTM system uses the equator as the reference. Northing coordinates are used in several grid systems. UTM, OSGB and MGRS are a few.

Off Course. A navigational statistics that tells you how far you are from the straight-line course between two points. It is usually reported as a distance to the right or the left of the straight-line course.

Outage. An outage occurs when the satellite geometry is so poor that the receiver cannot make an accurate position calculation. Most receivers will not lock when the position dilution of precision is greater than six.

Point-to-Point Calculation. The calculation of bearing and distance between two points.

Position Dilution of Precision (PDOP). See Dilution of Precision.

Precision Codes. The GPS satellites send two distinct signals: precision codes (P codes) and coarse acquisition codes (CA codes). Civilian receivers use the CA codes to determine position.

Military receivers use the CA codes to synchronize to the P codes before switching to the use of P code exclusively. During the time Selective Availability was used, it did not affect the P codes. The P codes are transmitted from space on two different frequencies, which enable military receivers to detect and illuminate propagation delays introduced in the ionosphere. The accuracy provided by the P codes is called the Precise Positioning Service (PPS).

Ranging. Ranging is the technique used in the GPS for a receiver to measure its distance to a satellite.

Route Function. A list of sequential waypoints. The GPS receiver guides you from the first waypoint on the list to each point in order until you arrive at the destination. See Goto Function.

RS-232. A standard type of connection to a computer. It is a serial port that allows communication between a computer and a receiver. A special cable connects the computer's RS-232 port to the receiver.

Satellite Geometry. The position of the satellites in the sky relative to your position on earth. The best satellite geometry is one satellite overhead with the others spread evenly around the horizon. See Dilution of Precision.

Selective Availability (SA). The techniques used by the U.S. Department of Defense to make civilian receivers less accurate. It limited horizontal accuracy to between 15 and 100 m (49.2 and 328 ft.) and vertical accuracy to 156 m (512 ft.). Selective Availability was eliminated May 2, 2000.

Speed of Advance (SOA). Same as VMG.

Speed Over Ground (SOG). The speed you are traveling regardless of direction. It is the same as ground speed.

Spoofing. Spoofing is a method of attacking the GPS to render it useless. The attacker transmits radio signals at the same frequency as the GPS signals so the receiver mistakes the fake signal for the real one and calculates an incorrect position. The countermeasure to spoofing is called anti-spoofing. Spoofing can be detected and foiled only by military receivers, not civilian ones.

Time to First Fix (TTFF). The amount of time (about 15 minutes) it takes a receiver to make its first position fix after it has been off for several months, lost memory or been moved more than 480 km (300 mi). Before the receiver can calculate its position, it needs to download all the position information about every satellite.

True North. The direction to the north pole. The north pole is not the magnetic pole. The difference in direction between the north pole and the magnetic pole is called declination.

Universal Polar Stereographic Grid (UPS). The grid that covers the Arctic and Antarctic regions. It is similar to UTM with eastings and northings.

Universal Serial Bus (USB). An electronic bus associated with computers. The USB allows a computer user to connect a GPS receiver or memory card programmer to a computer to transfer data. USB offers higher data rates than a computer's serial bus; so if you have a choice between a USB and a serial connection, select USB.

Universal Time Coordinated (UTC). Essentially Greenwich Mean Time. GPS time, as maintained by the satellites, is converted to UTC inside the receiver.

Universal Transverse Mercator Grid (UTM). The grid that splits the earth into 60 zones each of which is 6° wide. Its coordinates are relative to the equator and a zone meridian and are called eastings and northings. The UTM grid is used only between North 84° and South 80° because the UPS grid already provides a uniform grid for the poles.

Velocity Made Good (VMG). Your speed toward the destination. If you are traveling directly toward the destination, VMG is the same as your ground speed. If you are not on course, the VMG is less than your ground speed. If you are headed away from the destination, VMG is zero regardless of how fast you are going.

Waterproof. A receiver is listed as waterproof if it can be completely submerged in water without being ruined.

Water Resistant. A water-resistant receiver can be used in a damp environment, but it is not designed to be submerged or get really wet.

Waypoint. The coordinates of a location. Waypoints are stored in the receiver's memory. You can store your present position, as determined by the receiver, as a waypoint or you can store the position of any place in the world by reading its coordinates from a map and typing it into the receiver.

Wide Area Augmentation System (WAAS). Real-time DGPS corrections transmitted by satellites for use by receivers in the continental U.S., Alaska and parts of southern Canada. WAAS increases GPS receiver accuracy from 15 m (49.2 ft) to 3 m (9.8 ft.).

Y Code. The encrypted version of the P code. See Anti-Spoofing.

Resources

GPS Receiver Manufacturers
- Brunton (800) 443-4871, www.brunton.com
- Garmin International (800) 800-1020, www.garmin.com
- Magellan Systems (909) 394-5000, www.magellangps.com
- Lowrance Electronics (918) 437-6881, www.lowrance.com

GPS Computer Software
- DeLorme (800) 452-5931

Non-Map Software
- GPS Utility, www.gpsu.co.uk
- Mac GPS, www.macgpspro.com
- OziExplorer, www.oziexplorer.com

Computer, PDA and Pocket PC based Electronics Maps
- TOPO!, National Geographic, www.nationalgeographic.com/topo/
- Terrain Navigator, Terrain Navigator Pro, Pocket Navigator, Outdoor Navigator, Marine Navigator, MapTech, (888) 839-5551, www.maptech.com

Map Rulers
- Topo Companion, The Coordinator (800) 275-7526
- UTM Grid Reader (860) 243-0303
- The Card (for UTM grids) (800) 305-0036

GPS Systems for PDA and Pocket PC
- Navman USA, Inc., (603) 577-9600, (866) 628-6261, www.navman.com.
- Pharos, (310) 212-7088, www.pharosgps.com

Electronic Altimeters
- Avocet (650) 321-8501
- Casio (973) 361-5400

Third Party Mounting Solutions
- www.ram-mount.com

Other Books

Some basic map and compass books:

Staying Found: The Complete Map and Compass Handbook, 2nd ed., June Fleming, The Mountaineers, 1994

The Basic Essentials of Map and Compass, 2nd ed., Cliff Jacobson, ICS Books, 1997

Be Expert with Map and Compass: The Complete Orienteering Handbook, Bjorn Kjellstrom, MacMillan General Reference, 1994

Outward Bound Map and Compass Handbook, Glenn Randall, The Lyons Press, 1989

How to Read a Map (Using and Understanding Maps), Scott E. Morris, Chelsea House Publishers, 1993

An excellent book of map sources for maps all over the world is:
The Map Catalog: Every Kind of Map and Chart on Earth and Even Some Above It, 3rd ed., Joel Makower, editor; Vintage Books, 1992

Some heavy-duty books about mapmaking and GPS:

Map Use: Reading, Analysis, and Interpretation, Phillip C. Muehrcke, JP Publications, 1986

Global Positioning System: Theory and Practice, 2nd ed., B. Hofmann-Wellenhof et al., Springer-Verlag, 1997

The Navstar Global Positioning System, Tom Logsdon, Van Nostrand Reinhold, 1992

Understanding the Navstar: GPS, GIS and IVHS, Tom Logsdon, Van Nostrand Reinhold, 1995

A fine book about Amerigo Vespucci. It is short, but interesting.
Forgotten Voyager: The Story of Amerigo Vespucci, Ann Fitzpatrick Alper, Carolrhoda Books, 1991.

At the time of publication, the following Internet address was a good source of GPS information:
http://www.colorado.edu/geography/gcraft/notes/gps/gps_f.html

Index